POETRY SINCE 1939

By

STEPHEN SPENDER

Illustrated

Published for

THE BRITISH COUNCIL

by LONGMANS GREEN & CO

LONDON   NEW YORK   TORONTO

LONGMANS, GREEN AND CO. LTD.
6 & 7 CLIFFORD STREET, LONDON, W.1
NICOL ROAD, BOMBAY, 1
17 CHITTARANJAN AVENUE, CALCUTTA, 13
36A MOUNT ROAD, MADRAS, 2

LONGMANS, GREEN AND CO. INC.
55 FIFTH AVENUE, NEW YORK, 3

LONGMANS, GREEN AND CO.
215 VICTORIA STREET, TORONTO, 1

LONGMANS' CODE NUMBER : 10034

THIS BOOKLET IS PRODUCED IN
COMPLETE CONFORMITY WITH THE
AUTHORISED ECONOMY STANDARDS

C

BRITISH COUNCIL'S CODE NAME : POETRY (ENGLISH)

First published 1946

PRINTED IN GREAT BRITAIN
BY R. & R. CLARK, LIMITED, EDINBURGH

CONTENTS

ACKNOWLEDGEMENTS

The author and publishers are indebted to the following for permission to reprint poems which are quoted in full or at length: Mr. W. H. Auden and Messrs. Faber & Faber Ltd. for " Song of the Master and Boatswain ", from *For the Time Being*; Mr. George Barker and Messrs. Faber & Faber Ltd. for " To My Mother ", from *Eros in Dogma*; Mr. Ronald Bottrall and The Grey Walls Press Ltd. for " Peace "; Mr. David Gascoyne and Editions Poetry London for " The Gravel-Pit Field ", from *Poems 1939–42*; Mr. William Empson and Messrs. Faber & Faber Ltd. for " Missing Dates ", from *The Gathering Storm*; Mr. Roy Fuller and The Hogarth Press for " What is Terrible ", from *A Lost Season*; Mr. Robert Graves and Messrs. Cassell & Co. for " Dawn Bombardment " and " The Shot ", from *Poems 1938–1945*; Mr. Sidney Keyes and Messrs. George Routledge & Sons Ltd. for " Office for Noon ", from *The Cruel Solstice*; Mr. Laurie Lee and The Hogarth Press for " At Night ", from *The Sun My Monument*; Mr. Cecil Day Lewis and Messrs. Jonathan Cape Ltd. for " Where are the War Poets? " and " O Dreams, O Destinations " (second sonnet), from *Word Over All*; Mr. Louis MacNeice and Messrs. Faber & Faber Ltd. for " Brother Fire ", from *Springboard*; Mr. Edwin Muir and Messrs. Faber & Faber Ltd. for " Then " and " The Wayside Station ", from *The Narrow Place*; Mr. F. T. Prince and Editions Poetry London for " Soldiers Bathing "; Miss Kathleen Raine and Editions Poetry London for " Still Life ", from *Stone and Flower*; Mr. Henry Reed and Messrs. Jonathan Cape Ltd. for " The Door and the Window ", from *A Map of Verona*; Miss Edith Sitwell and Messrs. Macmillan & Co. Ltd. for " Anne Boleyn's Song ", from *Green Song*; Mr. Stephen Spender and Messrs. Faber & Faber Ltd. for " Since we are what we are, what shall we be . . . ", from *Spiritual Explorations*; Mr. Dylan Thomas and Messrs. J. M. Dent & Sons Ltd. for " Poem in October ", from *Deaths and Entrances*; Mr. Vernon Watkins and Messrs. Faber & Faber Ltd. for " The Sunbather ", from *The Ballad of the Mari Lwyd*.

POETRY SINCE 1939

In liberated Europe, and in other countries where, during the war, few English books have penetrated and little first-hand information about the Arts in Great Britain has been available, many people have asked, What has Britain produced during these five years? How has the impact of war influenced painters, musicians, writers, those whose minds are best able to penetrate below the surface and offer some clue to the world's chaos?

Stephen Spender has in this essay answered the question as regards Poetry. He is able to speak with double authority—as a poet, and as a one-time member of the National Fire Service, in which capacity he played his part in putting out the fires of London during the war. In writing of other poets, Stephen Spender was asked to include reference to his own work, which he has done in its proper place. But the Editor wishes to take this opportunity of reminding readers that the author of this essay is one of the most distinguished of our younger poets in England today.

TO
HENRI HELL
SOUVENIR OF PARIS
IN JUNE 1945

ILLUSTRATIONS

* From *The Poet's Eye*, an Anthology edited by
Geoffrey Grigson (Frederick Muller)

POETRY SINCE 1939

I. INTRODUCTORY

DURING the war every country in the world has been barred
off more or less completely from every other country. We
in Britain have been ignorant of what books have been written on
the continent during the last five years. It would be of the greatest
interest to read an account of European fiction or poetry during
this time.

For the same reason there is much curiosity in the countries of
Europe about the development of literature in war-time over here.
This book is written simply to answer the question " What poems
have been written between 1939 and 1945 in Britain?" This is an
important question which needs answering, because many people
have not had the opportunity to find out the answer for themselves.
I write about poetry in war-time to provide this information and
to endeavour to be a useful critical guide, drawing attention at
least to some books which are important. What is furthest from
my intention is to produce the impression that the poetry written
in war-time is different, as poetry, from the poetry written at any
other time. My excuse for concentrating on these six years is
simply that many people interested in English literature are ignorant
of them, not that they are more significant than any other years in
English poetry. From a purely literary point of view, it would be
more interesting to discuss English poetry during a longer stretch
of time, but that would not fulfil the immediate need.

It will be necessary, however, occasionally to go back, in discussing, for example, the development of poets like T. S. Eliot and
Edith Sitwell, and it will be necessary also sometimes to refer to
the reaction of the poets to the war. But, on the whole, I shall
endeavour to judge the poems written during this period, simply
as poetic achievement.

II. CONDITIONS IN WHICH POETS
HAVE WORKED

First of all, it is necessary to note the conditions in which poets have worked during the war.

In principle, everyone in Britain was mobilised to take part in the war effort (this mobilisation is, in fact, likely to extend far beyond the war). Certain people were, however, exempt from mobilisation, on account of age, illness, or because they were in reserved occupations. Although some painters were reserved to paint war pictures, no poet was reserved for the purpose of writing war poetry or any other kind of poetry.

It would be impossible, of course, for a poet to enter into an undertaking to write poetry about war in the same way that a painter can paint scenes of war. It would also have been impossible for a government in conducting total war to give poets complete freedom without any obligation to write propaganda or, indeed, to write anything: for these are the conditions of freedom which most poets require. Therefore poets have no grievance that they were " called up " like everyone else. Yet a deplorable waste and misuse and destruction of poetic talent is inevitably part of the expense of modern warfare, and it is hardly compensated for by the fact that the war stimulated much indiscriminate writing and publishing of poetry.

An inevitable result of the call-up was that the best poems written were by older men and women whom the war effort almost passed over, if it did not entirely do so. (T. S. Eliot was a part-time Air Raid Warden, Edwin Muir an administrator in Edinburgh of the British Council.) Some of the best poems written in these years were by T. S. Eliot, Edith Sitwell, Edwin Muir and Laurence Binyon.

W. H. Auden went to America in the autumn of 1938 and stayed there. His two books, *New Year Letter* and *For the Time Being*, show, if one compares them with the work of his contemporaries in England, that his American freedom enabled him to improve his technique enormously, so that he is now the most accomplished technician writing poetry in the English language.

The practical effect of the war on other English poets has been to turn them into administrators, government officials, soldiers, sailors, pilots; and to single a few out as pacifists and rebels.

The generation of poets who attracted much attention in the 1930's, Cecil Day Lewis, Louis MacNeice, William Empson, Spender and others, have tended to become officials: Day Lewis was employed in the Ministry of Information; William Plomer in the Admiralty; Louis MacNeice was a script writer in the B.B.C.; William Empson worked in the Far Eastern section of the B.B.C.; Arthur Waley, the distinguished translator of Chinese poems, worked in the Far Eastern section of the Ministry of Information. Spender was for some years a fireman, and later became a small hack of a war-time branch of the Foreign Office. Dylan Thomas was employed in documentary films.

Then we come to the many poets in the Forces. Some of the most talented of these were killed, notably Sidney Keyes and Alun Lewis. In quantity, the poets in the Forces produced far more work than anyone else, and, apart from the writing of distinguished poets such as Vernon Watkins, F. T. Prince, Roy Fuller, Henry Treece, Alan Rook, Keidrych Rhys, Francis Scarfe, this poetry is the most difficult to judge at the present time while we are so close to it.

Women poets fall into a rather special category. Apart from Miss Edith Sitwell, four outstanding women writers, Kathleen Raine, Anne Ridler, Ruth Pitter and E. J. Scovell, produced books during the war. When I come to review their work, it will be seen that their strength lies in their developing that peculiar branch of extremely sensitive and perceptive writing in which women can excel.

The pacifist poets have produced a small but vociferous literature which is too full of protest and self-justification to have much value. The most notable pacifist writer is Alex. Comfort, who is one of the most striking young talents in Britain.

The paper shortage and the situation in publishing play an

important part in the conditions of writers in war-time. After June 1940 paper suddenly became very scarce, newspapers were cut down to one-eighth of their size before the war, and publishers were limited to a quota of paper based on a small percentage of their pre-war consumption. Paper rationing was a hardship, but its results were not altogether bad. Most publishers behaved with a sense of responsibility towards literature and produced books of high quality, denying themselves paper for more popular work. Despite paper rationing, the sales of poetry increased, and even less-known poets could reckon their sales as between 2,000 and 4,000 instead of in hundreds, as would have been their circulation before the war.

III. CONDITIONS OF BRITISH POETS IN WAR COMPARED WITH THOSE OF POETS IN EUROPE

The war has been very different for British poets from the war on the continent for their European colleagues. For us in Britain the war has been a problem of distributing our resources of man-power and goods to meet the steadily increasing pressure of demands put on us by the war. We had no Occupation, no overwhelming catastrophe, no situation which it was impossible to meet.

In a sense we have gained by the war. We have learned to bring our virtues of courage, comradeship and citizenship forward into the open to put them at the service of a national cause. However, the values of imagination which cannot be related to public action, human personality considered apart from civic consciousness, beauty, romantic love, have suffered the neglect which is inevitable in a completely mobilised and conscripted community.

The situation on the continent in the Occupied Countries has been the very opposite of this. There, the German invasion, the Liberation and the ensuing chaotic conditions have produced situations which could not possibly be solved by the fair distribution of material resources in a moral climate of civic responsibility. The leaders of the Resistance Movements not only had to act but also they could think; and also they had leisure (not pleasant leisure, but nevertheless leisure) to learn the human lessons and the poetic values of their experiences. In such war poetry as England has produced, the intellectual acceptance of a necessary unity on the plane of material action is altogether different from the unity at a personal as well as an ardently patriotic level which we find in the French, the Czech, the Greek, the Norwegian, poetry of Resistance.

Yet although one may detect in English poetry of these years the haunting presence of a lament which is really for the lost and neglected freedom of emotion and imagination, nevertheless our poetry should prove to possess qualities that can supplement and fertilise the poetry of the continent and the world.

In their recent literary tradition the British have less reason to be ashamed of their poetry than of any branch of their literature. Moreover, many of the experiences of these years have been crystallised in poems, and many readers in Europe and also elsewhere in the world have a genuine hunger for an understanding of these experiences. In every country in Europe there is a great demand to know " what has been written " in other countries during the war. Ultimately this is a demand to know what the most perceptive and sensitive people, those most acutely endowed with the sense of life and the sense of love, have to say about our situation. Perhaps this demand is, from a literary point of view, not entirely " pure ", but nevertheless it seems to me to be natural and human, so I shall try to answer it, while at the same time keeping to the forefront literary values.

IV. T. S. ELIOT'S "FOUR QUARTETS"

Most critics would agree that the outstanding poetry produced in this war is contained in the *Four Quartets* of T. S. Eliot. This is a collection of four poems each of which has been published separately under the titles *Burnt Norton*, *East Coker*, *The Dry Salvages*,

Little Gidding. These poems are a series of meditations on ideas connected with time and timelessness. They have something in common with the Spiritual Exercises of the great mystics. Eliot takes as his starting point of the first poem *(Burnt Norton)* a hypothesis as to the nature of time:

> Time present and time past
> Are both perhaps present in time future,
> And time future contained in time past.
> If all time is eternally present
> All time is unredeemable.

Surely no other great poem in literature has opened on such a tentative note as this. The word " perhaps " in the second line excludes the possibility that this poem is a revelation, a vision, an assertion. It is a search for truth based on an exploration of conjectures about the mystery of time. Freedom from time does not lie in the pursuit of a future which is

> an abstraction
> Remaining a perpetual possibility
> Only in a world of speculation,

but in the attainment of a stillness which is outside time, a silence which succeeds speech:

> Only by the form, the pattern,
> Can words or music reach
> The stillness, as a Chinese jar still
> Moves perpetually in its stillness.

We must search for a plane where " all is always now ", a plane where we are freed from desire which binds us to time.

The thought of the *Four Quartets* is so closely knit as to defy paraphrase. Yet the *Four Quartets* are not abstract poetry, though they contain passages of thin-drawn abstraction. The names of places with significant pious associations which provide the titles of the poems, invoke the earth, lives lived in flesh and bone and stone, deeply rooted traditions. The intensity of exploration is relieved by passages of beautiful invocative description, such as the transparent account of a midwinter with which *Little Gidding* opens :

> Midwinter spring is its own season
> Sempiternal though sodden towards sundown,
> Suspended in time, between pole and tropic.
> When the short day is brightest, with frost and fire,
> The brief sun flames the ice, on pond and ditches,
> In windless cold that is the heart's heat,
> Reflecting in a watery mirror
> A glare that is blindness in the early afternoon.
> And glow more intense than blaze of branch, or brazier,
> Stirs the dumb spirit: no wind, but pentecostal fire
> In the dark time of the year.

Another theme of the *Four Quartets* is an (at times sententious) exploration of the poet's artistic conscience and of his own life. This volume is more self-revelatory of Eliot as man and as artist than his previous poetry.

Eliot uses words as precisely as a scientist or philosopher should use them. He does not use them to produce blurred impressionist effects, nor to create a personal language of his own isolated from the general prosaic use of language. There is no short cut to explain what these poems mean. They must be read line by line, and only thus can we understand what they say. However, let me emphasise again that Eliot's method is not that of argument, it is of search and exploration into the moment of the consciousness of human individuals who are capable of suddenly perceiving a pattern within events, a pattern which has the significance of a reality always present, though it is contained within a world in which future succeeds to the past, in which the idea of a point in time called " now " is entirely fictitious.

The time-theme of Eliot's poem is real exactly as birth, death and love are real, in fact as they are the only important realities. He makes us conscious of that which in the pursuit of our individual or our collective or our national or international aims we forget —the reality of our situation as living points of consciousness within life. In a sense the only aim in life which has any reality is

> A lifetime burning in every moment
> And not the lifetime of one man only
> But of old stones that cannot be deciphered.

The insistence on this reality created as poetic experience in a dozen or twenty different forms is the basic theme of the *Four Quartets*. Above this, though, there is a certain argument of high seriousness; in a passage recalling the words of St. John of the Cross he writes that

> In order to arrive there,
> To arrive where you are, to get from where you are not,
> You must go by a way wherein there is no ecstasy.
> In order to arrive at what you do not know
> You must go by a way which is the way of ignorance.
> In order to possess what you do not possess
> You must go by the way of dispossession.
> In order to arrive at what you are not
> You must go through the way in which you are not.

Four Quartets has been criticised as " escapist " literature. If my purpose in this essay were purely literary criticism, I should disdain to discuss this criticism, but I am writing partly for an audience which looks to poets for social as well as spiritual food, and I think that they must be answered, unless they are to regard much modern poetry as stones offered instead of bread.

Struggles to overthrow tyranny, to achieve social justice, to mitigate the suffering of the millions of victims of our age, are important exigencies today and they are all as much " within time ", to use Eliot's words, as any selfish or ambitious action which is attached to the aims of this world. It has been argued, therefore, that Eliot preaches a kind of mysticism which recommends the aim of turning away from action against the cruelty and suffering of our time. The answer to this argument is that Eliot does not offer his readers a drug which can make them forget the evils of the world. He offers them a truth, a vivid and fuller realisation of the relationship of that moment of consciousness when the individual called " I " relates his moment which he calls " now " with the past and future. This truth does not exclude social action. Moreover,

T. S. ELIOT

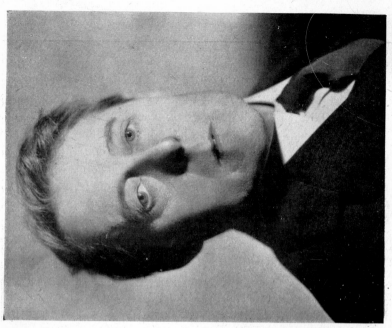

LAURENCE BINYON

MISS EDITH SITWELL

a reader who apprehended fully the reality of Eliot's poetry would, if he were influenced by this apprehension, sympathise more with his fellow-man and be less attached to the selfish desires which are the real cause of suffering in others.

On the other hand, it is true that Eliot is a writer so passionately attached to tradition that he cannot be regarded as on the side of social revolution. His tendency in his criticism and poetry is to regard everything untraditional as chaotic, empty and formless. He measures the tendencies of the modern world against what appears to him to be the solid rock of tradition, and finds his contemporaries men of straw, stuffed men, ghosts, hollow masks. Perhaps there is a lack of sympathy in his work for the hungry and the oppressed and for the aims of those who are trying to improve the material conditions of the world. Yet to say that his work is limited is different from saying that it is " escapist " and reactionary.

Eliot himself has claimed often in his creative writing that poetry has no social effects whatever, so that in his own view the above consideration would not concern him. In a recent essay on *The Man of Letters and the Future of Europe*, he considers that the Man of Letters only enters into social responsibilities in so far as there are times when " he is not as a rule exclusively engaged upon the production of works of art ". If we are living in an age in which past traditions have, in effect, been swept away by revolution, Eliot is a man who ignores that revolution, and this explains the great gap between his position and that of writers such as Eluard and Aragon. Despite all this, Eliot's is a voice which seems to speak for many of his contemporaries in Europe. His may well be the greatest poetic influence in the world today.

V. MISS EDITH SITWELL

Another poet whose work has shown a remarkable development during the war is Miss Edith Sitwell. Miss Sitwell's work first became famous in the 1920's when she began publishing at the same time as her two famous brothers, Osbert and Sacheverell. Her poetry had at this time a hard, brittle quality; it created a world inhabited by maid-servants, gardeners, ladies, all of them toylike characters in an artificial landscape which nevertheless had behind it the force of an obsessive personality. There were glimpses in her poetry of a deep tenderness and pity. In her later work she has developed her sympathy, though the theme of her poems is often a tragic frustration. In form her music is more melodious and the impression of a single poem is often of broad flowing sounds and lines which enclose an equally flowing imagery. In their flowing, golden richness, with their long lines like noble draperies, her poems often remind us of an oriental quality in the English imagination, produced by the influence of the Old Testament and pre-eminent in painters such as Samuel Palmer and William Blake. Her imagination is musical and pictorial and her inspiration emotive. There is none of the strained philosophic thought and search after philosophic truth of Eliot's later poetry.

During the war Miss Sitwell has published two volumes, *Street Songs* and *Green Song*. One is often carried away in these poems by the sheer beauty of the words and imagery in lines such as the following:

> I walk the world, envying the roads
> That have somewhere to go, that bear loads
>
> Of happiness, business and sorrow,
> And the rose that cares not for tomorrow.

The only way of conveying the vivid, mineral quality of these poems is to quote a whole poem. Here is one entitled *Anne Boleyn's Song*:

> " After the terrible rain, the Annunciation "—
> The bird-blood in the veins that has changed to emeralds
> Answered the bird-call . . .
> In the neoteric Spring the winter coldness
> Will be forgotten
> As I forget the coldness of my last lover,

The great grey King
Who lies upon my breast
And rules the bird-blood in my veins that shrieked with laughter
—A sound like fear—
When my step light and high
Spurned my sun down from the sky
In my heedless headless dance—
O many a year ago, my dear,
My living lass!

In the nights of Spring, the bird, the Angel of the Annunciation
Broods over his heaven of wings and of green wild-fire
That each in its own world, each in its egg
Like Fate is lying.

He sang to my blood, as Henry, my first King,
My terrible sun
Came like the Ethos of Spring, the first green streak,
And to me cried,
" Your veins are the branches where the first blossom begins
After the winter rains—
Your eyes are black and deep
As the prenatal sleep
And your arms and your breasts are my Rivers of Life
While a new world grows in your side."

Men said I was the primal Fall,
That I gave him the world of spring and of youth like an apple
And the orchards' emerald lore—
And sin lay at the core.

But Henry thought me winter-cold
When to keep his love I turned from him as the world
Turns from the sun . . . and then the world grew old—

But I who grew in the heart as the bird-song
Grows in the heart of Spring . . . I, terrible Angel
Of the emeralds in the blood of man and tree,
How could I know how cold the nights of Spring would be

When my grey glittering King—
Old amorous Death grew acclimatised to my coldness:
His age sleeps on my breast,
My veins, like branches where the first peach-blossom
Trembles, bring the Spring's warmth to his greyness.

Note in this poem the transparent jewel-like quality of the imagery, the tendency to transform the human feeling into something at first inhuman and then altogether cold and unfeeling. The blood of the queen first suggests bird-blood and then emeralds. This process of metamorphosis is interwoven with the association of spring, birds in branches and green leaves. The polar opposites, heat and cold, sun and earth, life and death, dominate the poem. At the same time a rare and aristocratic quality of imagination convinces us that this poem is indeed about a king and a queen. Altogether this is an extraordinary poetry, a poetry which no one except Miss Sitwell could have written.

VI. OTHER POETS OF AN ELDER GENERATION

Several other distinguished poets of a generation already famous in 1920 have published books in this war. In this brief survey I wish to draw the reader's attention to developments which are new and unfamiliar. In recent work, Edmund Blunden, Walter de la Mare, Siegfried Sassoon, Robert Graves and Masefield, each develops his particular gifts in the way that the reader of his works before the war would have anticipated.

If there are no new developments here—such as we find in Eliot, Edith Sitwell and Auden—there is work of admirable beauty. Blunden has made a quiet place for himself in English literature which he will always retain, and if his pastoral poetry is a byway, then there are byways in our literature which are and always have been very close to the main tradition. Along these sunlit paths, occasionally shadowed by poplars of a river on which gleam king-fishers, there were once the Elizabethan song-writers, once the

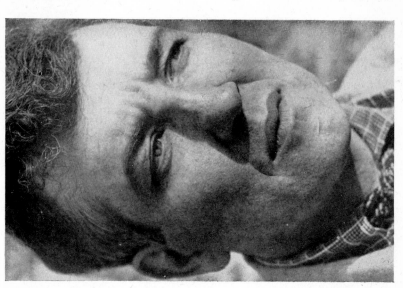

Robert Graves

Edwin Muir

ARTHUR WALEY

HERBERT READ

cavalier poets, once Christina Rossetti, and now there have been Blunden, Stanley Snaith and Walter de la Mare; and W. H. Davies has only recently departed.

Blunden's *Shells by a Stream* contains exquisite lyrics, occasionally marred by a too vague luminosity, a floating azure airiness to which he rises too easily:

> Above me crowns of cloud and thrones of light
> Moved with the minutes, and the season's blue,
> Autumn's soft raiment, veiled some forms of dream
> Which I yet reverence.

At times Blunden is master of a music and a pattern which is present in the best of Shelley, and which amongst more recent poets seems a secret of lightness and springing rhythm almost lost. Another older poet—surely one of Blunden's masters—who has the same traditional mastery is Walter de la Mare, whose *Collected Poems* were published during the war. De la Mare's writing has the rare quality of a nature which inhabits a world of poetry. The sharpest and most concrete experiences of his poems read like contacts with poetic and not real objects. His writing has the dreamlike quality not of the literary writer but of one for whom life is a dream. It is not that he lacks interest in real things but that he sees reality itself as filled with objects and characters of dreamlike significance.

Another older poet of great interest is Siegfried Sassoon, who, during the last war, was the most famous of the " disillusioned " war poets. Since the 1920's he has developed an idiosyncrastic personal poetry of vision of rare and fleeting moments of beauty, producing a concentrated and strangely ego-centric effect. Every experience centres on himself, his characteristic way of experiencing and expressing himself about it. *Rhymed Ruminations* is the appropriate half-ironic title of a new collection of these verses which always have the interest of Sassoon's own personality and odd isolation.

Blunden and Sassoon, these poets of the last war, are always interesting but their experience seems circumscribed, perhaps indeed by the influence of the war itself. One wonders whether the poets of this war will show similar qualities and similar limitations. Probably their development will be different because this war, with all its terrors, has been adventurous and expansive, more likely to produce agoraphobia than the claustrophobia of the war of 1914–1918.

Herbert Read, also a last-war soldier, has developed many interests in many directions, but his poetic gift, although genuine, has never enlarged to include his whole growth in thought and culture. His audience probably think of Read as a man of wide and exciting interests in aesthetics, general philosophy, literary criticism and politics, but as a limited poet. He has explored the reasons for his own limitations in a book called *Annals of Innocence and Experience*, which is a revealing study of the position of a modern poet in the modern world. His recent poems show the qualities of clear, hard imagery and intensely sincere expression, though they lack the compelling sense produced by an inevitable choice of words. Often one feels that he has worked hard to say something which might have been as well differently said. His poetry lacks compulsive inevitability. But Read is interesting in his poetry as in all his writings.

Two older poets produced distinguished work during the war. One was John Masefield, whose later poems seem conscientiously occasional (he is Poet Laureate), but which often contain rich and beautiful lines. In 1942 Masefield published a poem *The Land Workers*, which passed almost unnoticed amongst his official productions. It is a poem of mature, ripe, golden beauty, perhaps the crown of his achievement, recalling in many ways Goldsmith's *The Deserted Village*. It contains brilliant unforgettable pictures of country life in the England of Masefield's boyhood, made transparent by a sense of light and sadness, which have a great charm and purity:

> Under the earth those heroes are;
> Those Englishmen, slow, stubborn, kind,
> Who with odd gurgles, growls and clicks,
> Stacked the slain summer into ricks. . . .

The other poet of Masefield's generation who wrote well during these years was Laurence Binyon, art critic and scholar as well as poet, who wrote a few fine meditative poems which appeared in a posthumous collection, *The Burning of the Leaves*. He died in 1942. His greatest work in poetry was probably the magnificent translation of Dante into English *terza rima* completed by the *Paradiso* published in 1943. Richard Church is a quiet, sincere poet and novelist who published two volumes of poetry during the war—*The Solitary Man* and *A Twentieth Century Psalter*.

VII. ROBERT GRAVES

Robert Graves, a poet of the generation of Blunden and Sassoon, has shown a very marked development which isolates him from the other soldier poets of the last war. He writes a " pure " poets' poetry (he says in the Introduction to *Poems 1938–1945*: " To write poems for other than poets is wasteful "); a poetry which while retaining this quality of being " poets' poetry " also usually has as its starting point some common-sensical observation about daily experience: often to a single experience which might in itself seem insignificant and even trivial.

A short poem called *Dawn Bombardment* is a good example of his method of transforming an experience into poetry without the reader ever losing touch with the concreteness of the underlying everyday actuality. A scene of the firing of coastal guns at the beginning of the war is interpreted as a release of the mind from a long-pent-up nightmare of apprehension (this poem, by the way, is a significant revelation of the mind of a poet of the war of 1914–1918):

Dawn Bombardment

Guns from the sea open against us:
The smoke rocks bodily in the casemate
And a yell of doom goes up.
We count and bless each new, heavy concussion—
Captives awaiting rescue.

> Visiting angel of the wild-fire hair
> Who in dream reassured us nightly
> Where we lay fettered,
> Laugh at us, as we wake—our faces
> So tense with hope the tears run down.

This is as good an example as one could wish of a certain characteristic poetic method—the translation of an experience into dream, or rather the establishment of an identity between dream and its fulfilment in an experience.

A poem which illustrates the high degree of originality which Graves can achieve in language is *The Shot*:

> The curious heart plays with its fears:
> To hurl a shot through the ship's planks,
> Being assured that the green angry flood
> Is charmed and does not dance into the hold—
> Nor first to sweep a lingering glance around
> For land or shoal or cask adrift.
> "So miracles are done; but madmen drown."
>
> O weary luxury of hypothesis—
> For human nature, honest human nature
> (Which the fear-pampered heart denies)
> Knows its own miracle: not to go mad.
> Will pitch the shot in fancy, hint the fact,
> Will bore perhaps a meagre auger hole
> But stanch the spurting with a tarred rag,
> And will not drown, nor even ride the cask.

The poet is concerned here with the contrast between the mind's exaggerated fantasies and the comparative sanity of ordinary behaviour. It is a simple translation of a commonplace of observation into the most vivid language of poetic experience. This combination of ordinariness with extraordinary freshness gives Graves's poetry a stubborn, natural, honest, wizened quality like that of a tree growing in an orchard.

The great virtues of Graves are his lack of pretentiousness and his truth to his own way of thinking. By implication Graves's poems are an ironic comment on the more exalted poetic ambitions of most of his contemporaries. Characteristically, Graves dislikes Virgil, Milton and nearly all " great " attempts in poetry. Poetically, he lives very strictly within his means and he is shrewdly aware of the overdrafts on their talents of many of his contemporaries.

VIII. EDWIN MUIR

The work of one rather neglected poet has shown a development during the war almost as marked as that of T. S. Eliot and Edith Sitwell. This is Edwin Muir. Edwin Muir is a Scottish writer whose early life on a remote island in the Orkneys is beautifully described in his *The Story and the Fable*, an autobiography which will live in English literature as a minor classic. He is also well known as the translator of Franz Kafka. Muir, like Eliot, is obsessed with the idea of time. But whereas in Eliot there is the search to put oneself outside time by the path of dispossessing oneself of aims and preoccupations which are worldly and therefore carried away by it, Muir is fascinated by contemplation of the stream of time itself:

> The disciplined soldiers come to conquer nothing,
> March upon emptiness and do not know
> Why all is dead and life has hidden itself.
> The enormous winding frontier walls fall down,
> Leaving anonymous stone and vacant grass.
> The stream flows on into what land, what peace,
> Far past the other side of the burning world?

A poem called *Then* fixes the attention on the achievement of human generations which is a stain of blood on a wall:

> There were no men and women then at all,
> But the flesh lying alone,
> And angry shadows fighting on a wall
> That now and then sent out a groan
> Buried in lime and stone,
> And sweated now and then like tortured wood
> Big drops that looked yet did not look like blood.

And yet as each drop came a shadow faded
And left the wall.
There was a lull
Until another in its shadow arrayed it,
Came, fought and left a blood-mark on the wall;
And that was all; the blood was all.

If there had been women there they might have wept
For the poor blood, unowned, unwanted,
Blank as forgotten script.
The wall was haunted
By mute maternal presences whose sighing
Fluttered the fighting shadows and shook the wall
As if that fury of death itself were dying.

A poem called *The Human Fold* contemplates the human situation:

There's no alternative here but love,
So far as genuine love can be. . . .

The Wheel, The Law, The City, The Grove, The Fate—such titles
suggest readily the subjects of Mr. Muir's poetry.

In these poems Edwin Muir emphasises a tendency in modern
poetry which is more significant than the somewhat heady and self-
lacerating movement of surrealists and apocalyptics. This is the
submission of the poet, heart and soul, to the contemplation of
the poetry of reality, the primitive facts of the human situation in
the universe. Emotionally it is an appeal away from the loudly
proclaimed aims of human societies and individuals back to the
bare facts of human existence. Poetically it is (like Eliot's later
poems) a return to the great subjects of poetry, love, death, time—
the great subjects which write their own poetry through the medium
of the poet who cares more for truth than for the expression of
his own personality and the advertisement of his own power over
words.

The words here are unobtrusive of the writer's own personality,
submissive to his theme. It must be admitted that Muir is often
awkward in his choice of words, his form sometimes seems arbi-

trarily chosen as a vessel in which to pour a poem; it does not grow from the subject like the leaves from the bough of a tree. In the second passage I have quoted above, the line " Until another in its shadow arrayed it " is awkward, and not strengthened by the fact that " arrayed it " is supposed to rhyme with " faded ". Nevertheless, sometimes Muir writes a completely successful poem, a poem which, when one has read it once, seems to become a part of one's life, because it expresses so exactly an experience and a sequence of thought which is the rhythm of the eye, the ear and the mind. Such a poem is *The Wayside Station*:

> Here at the wayside station, as many a morning,
> I watch the smoke torn from the fumy engine
> Crawling across the field in serpent sorrow.
> Flat in the east, held down by stolid clouds,
> The struggling day is born and shines already
> On its warm hearth far off. Yet something here
> Glimmers along the ground to show the seagulls
> White on the furrows' black unturning waves.
>
> But now the light has broadened.
> I watch the farmstead on the little hill,
> That seems to mutter: " Here is day again "
> Unwillingly. Now the sad cattle wake
> In every byre and stall,
> The ploughboy stirs in the loft, the farmer groans
> And feels the day like a familiar ache
> Deep in his body, though the house is dark.
> The lovers part
> Now in the bedroom where the pillows gleam
> Great and mysterious as deep hills of snow,
> An inaccessible land. The wood stands waiting
> While the bright snare slips coil by coil around it,
> Dark silver on every branch. The lonely stream
> That rode through darkness leaps the gap of light,
> Its voice grown loud, and starts its winding journey
> Through the day and time and war and history.

IX. W. H. AUDEN AND THE POETS OF THE
'THIRTIES

In the 'thirties there was a group of poets who achieved a very
wide reputation as a " school " of modern poetry.   They were not
in a deliberate sense a literary movement; they were rather a group
of friends, contemporaries at the Universities of Oxford and Cambridge, influenced by each other in a personal way.   The chief
influence was undoubtedly the powerful intelligence and personality
of W. H. Auden.   Thus they had certain ideas in common.   They
consciously attempted to be modern, choosing in their poems
imagery selected from machinery, slums and the social conditions
which surrounded them.   They showed a tendency to be swamped
in their sensibility by the sense of the world in which they found
themselves.   Their poetry emphasised the community, and, overwhelmed as it was by the sense of a communal disease, it searched
for a communal cure in psychology and leftist politics.   Their
personal emotions, although they were present, lacked finality for
them in a modern world in which they foresaw many of the social
evils which subsequently overtook the world.   Despite an almost
exhibitionistic attitude towards sex, these poets rather lacked
sensuality, and their approach to all problems was very intellectual.
At the same time, they could be criticised for not immersing themselves completely in social problems and in the contemplation of
disaster.   Their poetry often gives the impression that they stayed
at the fringe of their own personalities and of the problems which
obsessed them.   To a great extent, their poetry, though leftist,
expresses the problem of the liberal divided between his individual
development and his social conscience.

When all this is said, W. H. Auden, Day Lewis, MacNeice,
Spender, Lehmann and the others of this phase of poetry are
interesting because their work expresses a malaise which shows a
moral conscience more sensitive than that of many of their contemporaries.   They may even claim to have written, during the

CECIL DAY LEWIS

LOUIS MACNEICE

W. H. Auden

Stephen Spender

Spanish Civil War, the English poetry of a just democratic war against Fascist tyranny.   Auden's *Spain*, Day Lewis's *Nabara*, some passages of MacNeice's *Autumn Journal*, some poems of Spender in *The Still Centre*, are the climax of this phase, when, in the Spanish conflict, these poets at last seemed to have found a cause in which their liberal values were fused with a public issue.   W. H. Auden, MacNeice and Spender all went to Spain during the war, whilst Ralph Fox, Julian Bell, Christopher Caudwell and John Cornford all played an heroic part with the International Brigade.   Fox, Bell, Caudwell and Cornford were killed in this first war for democracy in Europe.

Just before this war W. H. Auden, the most brilliant poet of his generation in England, went to New York.   Here he continued to write the didactic, highly intellectualised, technically dazzling, at times wise poetry of an aloof commentator, endowed with great cleverness and a lucid gift.   Auden's peculiar strength is perhaps to see the symbolic and psychological aspect of everything.   He can pass a magic wand over a landscape or a crowd and endow every person and object with a significant place in the struggle of existence.   Thus he writes from America to England in *New Year Letter*:

> I can but think our talk in terms
> Of images that I have seen,
> And England tells me what we mean.
> Thus, squalid beery *Burton* stands
> For shoddy thinking of all brands,
> The wreck of *Rhondda* for the mess
> We make when for a short success
> We split our symmetry apart . . .

This gift for labelling everyone and everything with an effective epithet reduces morality, love, illness, politics, the literary figures of the past, all to the same level of counters in Auden's mind:

> Conscious *Catullus*, who made all
> His gutter-language musical,
> Black *Tennyson*, whose talents were
> For an articulate despair,
> Trim, dualistic Baudelaire . . .

No poet since Pope has approached every problem with the same confidence that he has the light, the power, all the instruments necessary to dissect and label every phenomenon and relate it to every other phenomenon.

Several critics—notably Geoffrey Grigson and Kathleen Raine—have drawn attention to Auden's knowledge of the human heart. He has great gifts of understanding and sympathy and his poetry is full of observations which are profound and true. Yet he lacks respect for the irredeemable mystery of a concrete reality which is inseparable from the nature of things in themselves. His poetry at times produces the impression that he uses a poetic language to assist himself in the search for a formula which would explain the nature of life.

These faults—if they are faults—are inherent in didactic poetry and they do not detract from Auden's being a great intellectual poet of our time. Moreover, there are situations in which his qualities are at their happiest and his writing suddenly has a calm and beautiful relation to his subject. The first of two poems in a volume called *For the Time Being* contains the best of Auden's poetry since his journey to America. This poem is a series of recitatives by the characters of Shakespeare's *Tempest*, who are supposed to have left the magic island and to be returning to Milan. To Auden, *The Tempest* has always appeared to be the mystery play in which Shakespeare came nearest to expressing his philosophy in characters who have a symbolic significance. Thus Ariel is interpreted by Auden, not as a puckish spirit but as an attitude having an effect on other lives:

> For all things
> In your company, can be themselves: historic deeds
> Drop their hauteur and speak of shabby childhoods
> When all they longed for was to join in the gang of doubts
> Who so tormented them; sullen diseases
> Forget their dreadful appearance and make silly jokes;
> Thick-headed goodness for once is not a bore.

Auden is at his happiest in this commentary on Shakespeare. At least two of the situations are of a kind in which he is able to enter into a loving regard towards the characters, instead of only preaching love. The speech of Prospero to Ariel in which the philosopher, from his height of wisdom and resignation, addresses the wild spirit, is of great beauty, and this relationship of the older teacher to the masculine child is paralleled by the wonderfully sustained letter from Alonso to Ferdinand, advising him how to behave when he ascends to the throne. The song of master and boatswain which follows this letter is Auden at his most fantastic, humorous and strong:

> At Dirty Dick's and Sloppy Joe's
>   We drank our liquor straight,
> Some went upstairs with Margery,
>   And some, alas, with Kate;
> And two by two like cat and mouse
> The homeless played at keeping house.
>
> There Wealthy Meg, the Sailor's Friend,
>   And Marion, cow-eyed,
> Opened their arms to me but I
>   Refused to step inside;
> I was not looking for a cage
> In which to mope in my old age.
>
> The nightingales are sobbing in
>   The orchards of our mothers,
> And hearts that we broke long ago
>   Have long been breaking others;
> Tears are round, the sea is deep:
> Roll them overboard and sleep.

In addition to *New Year Letter* and *For the Time Being*, Auden also published during the war years a volume of miscellaneous poems, *Another Time*. This volume, with three sections, called People and Places, Lighter Poems and Occasional Poems, shows an occasional character. Many of the poems take the form of critical poetic analyses of people and their attitudes, or of places, such as Oxford, Brussels and Dover. There are poems about writers such as Edward Lear, A. E. Housman, Rimbaud, Herman Melville, Pascal, etc. Altogether the volume has a self-conscious rather impersonal character, though this is interrupted at moments by lyrics as beautiful as the famous one beginning:

> Lay your sleeping head, my love,
> Human on my faithless arm;
> Time and fevers burn away
> Individual beauty from
> Thoughtful children, and the grave
> Proves the child ephemeral:
> But in my arms till break of day
> Let the living creature lie,
> Mortal, guilty, but to me
> The entirely beautiful.

Even in such a poem as this one notices a degree of self-consciousness amounting to disillusion about the loved one. What Auden seems to be saying is "I know love is an illusion, and I know that I am wrong to think my love, who is mortal and guilty, to be beautiful. But still I welcome the illusion." Something like this is, indeed, the message of his latest poem *For the Time Being*. Yet it may seem to the reader that there is a further implication, not so openly stated, of Auden's attitude. Not only is he disillusioned about the loved one, but he is also superior. He is in the position to analyse the loved one and the situation of being in love, whereas the loved one is a mere victim of the situation.

Auden is certainly the dominating and outstanding talent among the poets who have been associated with him. He has an astonishing virtuosity both of form and idea; above all, he has the great gift of putting into words ideas and sensations which are extremely elusive. He has an eager intellectual curiosity and a great subtlety which makes him express ideas which seem never before to have had such subtlety and depth as when he experienced them. At times he seems to overreach himself: as when he sums up, all too neatly, in a sonnet the entire significance of Rimbaud or Housman.

It is illuminating to compare Auden with a writer whose qualities at first sight may appear almost the opposite of his: I mean, Rudyard Kipling. For Kipling is the poet of an almost fanatical patriotism, whereas it is well known that Auden left England shortly

Dylan Thomas

Vernon Watkins

David Gascoyne

George Barker

I'm working like a shoal.

before the war and, during the war, took out papers for American nationalisation. But it is their writing and not their actions which concerns us here. Auden, like Kipling, has an astonishing power of improvisation, of using any and every form for his own purposes, exquisitely, yet without giving the impression that he is specially attached to any form. His thought seems to be a liquid which flows readily into any and every shape. He has an almost disconcerting mastery of idiom: so much so that his longer pieces seem to disintegrate into their separate parts by entering too completely into the mood and idea of each part, without being held together by a central idea. He has a great mastery of modern techniques and of machinery. He is perfectly at home with any kind of technical—engineer's or psychologist's—jargon. Auden is the only other English poet whom one can conceivably imagine writing a poem which shows the masterly understanding and even sympathy for the machinery of a ship of Kipling's *M'Andrew's Hymn*. Above all, there is a certain elusiveness about the work of both Auden and Kipling which makes them both extremely difficult, in the last analysis, to appraise. It is easy to say what is Kiplingesque or Audenesque. But it is far more difficult to have a concrete grasp of a consistently developing Kipling or Auden in the work of each. This elusiveness gives the work of both an inexplicable and dazzling quality which one admires, because one cannot understand how it came to be created. The difference between trying to explain a poem by Eliot, say, and one by Auden is like that between trying to explain a crime with and one without an apparent motive. For although Eliot is not a " personal " poet, one is always aware of the presence of a living, human Eliot in his poetry. With Auden one is aware of the Audenesque mood and the Audenesque attitude and of much else besides: but not of Auden. His poetry therefore puzzles and eludes as much as it astonishes and attracts. The greatest poetry has such qualities of impersonality: so has the work of writers who have dazzled their contemporaries but failed to interest posterity. Myself, I think that Auden has qualities of greatness, but the critical question will be decided by other critics than I.

C

X. DAY LEWIS, MacNEICE AND SPENDER

The other poets of the 'thirties have continued to write during these years, but the war has been a period of reorientation for them in which their whole energies have not gone into the writing of poetry. This can be explained partly by circumstances which have denied almost everyone in Britain the time in which to pursue creative tasks. However, it is partly also to be explained by the doubt of these poets whether the war, which was certainly against Fascism, was for a purified cause. A poem by Day Lewis, written in answer to the cry sometimes taken up by the newspapers against the poets for not writing war poetry, expresses this situation:

Where are the War Poets?

They who in folly or mere greed
Enslaved religion, markets, laws,
Borrow our language now and bid
Us to speak up in freedom's cause.

It is the logic of our times,
No subject for immortal verse—
That we who lived by honest dreams
Defend the bad against the worse.

There was a tendency for the poetry of Day Lewis, MacNeice and Spender to turn inwards towards a personal subject matter and to avoid the world of outer events. MacNeice, whose style is always gay and polished, being modelled on the Latin poets who took their sorrows with a certain grace and lightness, wrote a series of love poems ironically entitled *The Last Ditch*, which was perhaps his most deliberately casual volume. Stephen Spender wrote the very introspective poems in search of a universal experience through subjective contemplation which form the last section of *Ruins and Visions*:

Structures are melted in a soft pond
Of darkness, up to the stars.

> Man's mind swims, full of lamps,
> Among foundations of the epoch.
> Clothes fade to the same curtains
> As night draws over the blaze of flesh.

Day Lewis concentrated on the perfection of a technique owing much to Thomas Hardy and to Irish ballads, in which he wrote some very effective pastoral love poems. He also made a magnificent translation of Virgil's *Eclogues*. His sequence of sonnets on childhood, entitled *O Dreams, O Destinations*, contained his best introspective writing:

> Children look down upon the morning-grey
> Tissue of mist that veils a valley's lap:
> Their fingers itch to tear it and unwrap
> The flags, the roundabouts, the gala day.
> They watch the spring rise inexhaustibly—
> A breathing thread out of the eddied sand,
> Sufficient to their day: but half their mind
> Is on the sailed and glittering estuary.
> Fondly we wish their mist might never break,
> Knowing it hides so much that best were hidden:
> We'd chain them by the spring, lest it should broaden
> For them into a quicksand and a wreck.
> But they slip through our fingers like the source,
> Like mist, like time that has flagged out their course.

The events of 1940, the Fall of France, the threat of invasion, the air raids on Britain, are reflected in the work of these poets. Day Lewis wrote a series of poems inspired by his activities in the Home Guard which, although they contain fine passages, suffer from the emotional uncertainty of a poet who is least sure of himself when he writes of his immediate feelings.

MacNeice, who returned to England from America during the Blitz, and who fire-watched in St. Paul's during some of the worst raids, wrote some heroic poems about the raids. These poems are greatly strengthened by the devil-may-care attitude towards events which occasionally make his poems appear facile. *Brother Fire*, one of this series, is a wonderful fusion of gaiety and tragedy.

It is such a poem as one might expect to hear from the lips of Don
Juan in Hell:

> When our brother Fire was having his dog's day
> Jumping the London streets with millions of tin cans
> Clanking at his tail, we heard some shadow say
> " Give the dog a bone "—and so we gave him ours;
> Night after night we watched him slaver and crunch away
> The beams of human life, the tops of topless towers.
>
> Which gluttony of his for us was Lenten fare
> Who mother-naked, suckled with sparks, were chill
> Though cotted in a grill of sizzling air
> Striped like a convict—black, yellow and red;
> Thus were we weaned to knowledge of the Will
> That wills the natural world but wills us dead.
>
> O delicate walker, babbler, dialectician Fire,
> O enemy and image of ourselves,
> Did we not on those mornings after the All Clear,
> When you were looting shops in elemental joy
> And singing as you swarmed up city block and spire,
> Echo your thought in ours? " Destroy!   Destroy! "

Springboard, a collection of MacNeice's poems 1941–1944, fore-
shadows a development in his work which it yet does not completely
fulfil. *Prayer before Birth*, which is the prayer for the soul of an
unborn child, is a passionate appraisal of the situation of the modern
world into which a child is born, at once an imprecation against
and a guide through the total State:

> I am not yet born, console me.
> I fear that the human race may with tall walls wall me,
>   with strong drugs dope me, with wise lies lure me,
>   on black racks rack me, in blood-baths roll me.

The Kingdom is an attempt to write a poem in honour of the
secret conspiracy of human beings to remain human throughout
life, people who retain their souls, those to whom Stendahl dedi-
cated his masterpiece under the secret and sacred inscription " To
the Happy Few ":

Under the surface of flux and of fear there is an underground movement,
Under the crust of bureaucracy, quiet behind the posters,
Unconscious but palpably there—the Kingdom of individuals.

This is a great idea for a poem (it is, again, one of the great
subjects which write themselves in the mind of a poet who submits
to them), but MacNeice does not succeed completely in creating
it imaginatively.   His poem declines into a list of examples drawn
from life of members of the Kingdom, instead of penetrating into
the innermost truth of existence which distinguishes the true from
the false, the living from the dead.

MacNeice's poetry fails to achieve a greatness it might attain, by
a certain casualness not so much of manner, as of feeling.   At times
this produces an inspired, even a heroic, effect: but when he is
trying to create an impression intense and yet massive—as in *The
Kingdom*—the emotion disintegrates.

Spender's sequence of poems entitled *Spiritual Explorations* is a
parallel attempt to penetrate the very nature of human existence.
I quote here the third sonnet:

> Since we are what we are, what shall we be
> But what we are?   We are, we have,
> Six feet and seventy years, to see
> The light, and then release it for the grave.
>   We are not worlds, no, nor infinity,
> We have no claims on stones, except to prove
> In the invention of the human city
> Our selves, our breath, our death, our love.
>   The tower we build soars like an arrow
> From the earth's rim into the sky's,
> Upwards and downwards in that blazing pond
> Climbing and diving from our life, to narrow
> The gap between the world shut in the eyes
> And the receding world of light beyond.

Day Lewis's *O Dreams, O Destinations*, MacNeice's *Prayer before
Birth* and Spender's *Spiritual Exercises* reveal the innermost development of these poets under the shadow of war.

XI. WILLIAM EMPSON AND OTHERS

William Empson, a Cambridge contemporary of Auden's Oxford contemporaries, is a highly intellectual writer whose poems are ambiguous and complicated. His best work is contained in a volume published during the war called *The Gathering Storm*, in which his subject matter and experience is enlarged on his earlier poetry by journeys to Japan and China and by his vision from the Far East of the storms which were gathering at the same time over Europe.

The extreme difficulty of Empson's poems, to understand which demands a more than ordinary knowledge of the English language and of modern scientific thought, puts them out of reach of the ordinary general reading public. Indeed it is difficult to postulate an ideal reader qualified to understand completely one of Empson's more difficult poems, for, in addition to his having to be a specialist in various branches of knowledge, he would also have to grasp the significance of references to obscure people and private events which can scarcely be known to any except Empson's closest associates. In the notes at the end of *The Gathering Storm* Empson helps the reader by elucidating some of these difficulties.

Despite all their difficulties and their occasional wilfulnesses, Empson's poems command the respect of a small circle of critically-minded people, and there are good reasons why they should do so. They are the poems of a man of great intellectual power, independent judgement and personal integrity, who, although he participates in experiences, does so with detachment, critically, and without losing himself in opinions or feelings outside himself.

Thus Empson's poetic personality is like a rock compared with the fluid amorphous chameleonic personality of Auden, whose work seems one long attempt on the part of the poet to lose himself in some formularised " solution " of his own inner problems, through socialism, psychology or anglicanism. A poem called *Ignorance of Death* is characteristic of Empson's intellectual awareness of a universal problem, his power of crystallising attitudes towards it and his refusal to associate himself with conventional attitudes towards a problem which is insoluble.   The poem ends:

> Because we have neither hereditary nor direct knowledge of death
> It is the trigger of the literary man's biggest gun
> And we are happy to equate it to any conceived calm.
>
> Heaven me, when a man is ready to die about something
> Other than himself, and is in fact ready because of that,
> Not because of himself, that is something clear about himself.
>
> Otherwise I feel very blank upon this topic,
> And think that though important, and proper for anyone to bring up,
> It is one that most people should be prepared to be blank upon.

Frequently in his poems Empson expresses a certain disdain for the communal impulse.   He realises that even a right cause may be vitiated by the complacent self-righteousness of people supporting it.   Here he is surely an acute critic of our time, in which it is particularly easy to have opinions which seem right, to belong to some movement which may have noble aims and which yet somehow still has ignoble supporters.   He realises that the emotions which go into supporting a good cause, although they may be necessary, do not strengthen the intellect and character of the individual who holds them:

> Besides, I do not really like
> The verses about " Up the Boys ",
> the revolutionary romp,

he explains in a poem in which nevertheless he approves of " the outcry over the Hoare-Laval pact and the swing-round of the Trade Unions to rearmament then ".   An eccentric and interesting personality is expressed in these poems.   They are written in a transparent language at once hard and clear, intellectual and cold-seeming, yet often burning with intensity.   Occasionally he produces lines of conventional beauty such as

> We have had the autumn here.   But oh
> That lovely balcony is lost

Just as the mountains take the snow.
The soldiers will come here and train.
The streams will chatter as they flow.

I quote in its entirety the poem *Missing Dates* because it is one of the easiest to understand and because it illustrates well the technical mastery of Empson. Note that this poet with all his complexity has a certain downrightness of utterance, and that his highly individual point of view is also common-sensical:

Slowly the poison the whole blood stream fills.
It is not the effort nor the failure tires.
The waste remains, the waste remains and kills.

It is not your system or clear sight that mills
Down small to the consequence a life requires;
Slowly the poison the whole blood stream fills.

They bled an old dog dry yet the exchange rills
Of young dog's blood gave but a month's desires;
The waste remains, the waste remains and kills.

It is the Chinese tombs and the slag hills
Usurp the soil, and not the soil retires.
Slowly the poison the whole blood stream fills.

Not to have fire is to be a skin that shrills.
The complete fire is death. From partial fires
The waste remains, the waste remains and kills.

It is the poems you have lost, the ills
From missing dates, at which the heart expires.
Slowly the poison the whole blood stream fills.
The waste remains, the waste remains and kills.

Empson was the Cambridge contemporary of Auden, Day Lewis, MacNeice, Spender, when these were at Oxford. Other poets at Cambridge at the same time were Michael Roberts, Ronald Bottrall, Kathleen Raine, John Lehmann, Julian Bell (killed in Spain) and Charles Madge.

Ronald Bottrall, who has, like Empson, been in China, and who is now working for the British Council in Rome, is a poet of the same highly intellectual school as Empson. He has been much influenced by the work of Ezra Pound. His intellect lacks the transcendent qualities of Empson and often his poems are acute lively topical observations written in a consciously modern idiom.

His volume *Farewell and Welcome* contains love poems which have an intensity greater than that of his poems echoing Eliot and Pound but he does not seem to have fulfilled his early promise yet. One of Bottrall's most recent poems, although outside the period covered by this volume, well deserves quoting, because besides illustrating his work at its best, it shows the attitude of an English poet looking beyond the war to the peace, with a sidewards glance at the atomic bomb. It is called *Peace* :

> When may we expect peace? Not that false peace
> That masquerades between the troughs of seas,
> Deceives in the silence between earthquakes, or the lull
> Between atomic bombs. Peace is the pull
> Towards the motion of tree, star and stone,
> The contented rhythm of the child at the nipple,
> The moment of surrender after union.
> Peace is the stirlessness of a nesting bird,
> A tiptoeing on mountains with the sun,
> A flowering forward to the end of will
> And the joyful whispering of the timeless word
> That passeth understanding, bringing time's harvest home.
> Peace will come when there is no more murder in the womb.

Kathleen Raine is a poet of genuine intensity who writes poems which often have a hard gem-like transparency. Her volume *Stone and Flower* published in 1943 at once established her reputation. *Still Life* is an example of the pure effect which she can produce:

> The hour of sight,
> Flower of light
> And unendurable
> Wings of flight
>
> All turn to fossil,
> Turn to stone
> The delicate shell
> And the mighty bone.

The blood the nerves
The trace of thought
That cross the night
From the sources of the world.

The play of light
In the wake of the sun
Is suddenly still
Like a frozen stream

Suddenly still
Bird, flower and shell
That love has created,
Life-shaped and perfected,
So to remain.

Several other poets of this generation are of interest.   Eccentric but certainly important are John Betjeman's satiric yet devout, derisive yet serious, poems on the Church of England, vicarages, the tennis lawn, the suburbs.   Betjeman, too self-mocking to be serious, has made a serious and original medium of parody, imitation and the English tradition of " humorous verse ".   Great precision of form and extremely accurate and delicate observation put him with Blunden as a nature poet.

Intolerably sad, profound
St. Giles's bells are ringing round,
They bring the slanting summer rain
To tap the chestnut boughs again
Whose shadowy cave of rainy leaves
The gusty belfry song receives.

How beautiful here is the idea of the caves of darkness held under the boughs of trees.

Ann Ridler writes poems on Anglican and domestic themes which often contain sharply visualised and accurate passages of description and a pleasant sincerity of devout feeling.

E. J. Scovell and Lilian Bowes Lyon are two other women poets who bring to modern English poetry the subtle and fine sensibility which has been the peculiar contribution of women to our contemporary literature.

John Lehmann is a talented poet and his recent poems published in *The Sphere of Glass* have a richness and visionary quality which is a development on his work of the 'thirties. The pictorial quality of Lehmann's poetry, recalling the work of some of the later Victorian writers, often has charm and vividness, as in these lines from *The Sphere of Glass*:

> Within the wood, within that hour
> It seemed a sphere of glass had grown
> That glittered round their lives, with power
> To link what grief the dyke had known
> With voices of their vaster war
> The sun-shot bombers' homing drone,
>
> And make one tragic harmony
> Where still this theme, their hope, returned,
> And still the Spring unchangeably
> In fires of its own sap was burned,
> And poetry, from love and death,
> The peace their human contest earned.
>
> It might have been all history
> Without the sphere of wonder lay
> And just beyond their colloquy
> Some truth more pure than they could say,
> While through the bluebells and the fern
> Sister and brother made their way.

Another poet of charm and promise is Lawrence Durrell, whose poems in *A Private Country* reflect sensitively the influence of the Greek landscape and the Greek myth. Julian Symons, a communist writer, has concision and intelligence, but perhaps he is by nature a thinker in prose rather than a poet. He is an excellent critic of poetry.

Geoffrey Grigson, editor of the magazine *New Verse* which ceased publication at the beginning of the war, and an acute critic of his contemporaries, published a volume of poems, *Several Observations*, containing meticulous pictorial effects and one or two good translations from Hoelderlin and Rilke. I should mention here the excellent translations of Rilke done by John Leishmann, Michael Hamburger's translations of Hoelderlin, O. Sigler's translation of his young Czech contemporary Fred Marnau, Norman Cameron's translations of Rimbaud and also of Nesswald, Spender and Gili's translations of Lorca. In 1943 C. M. Bowra published another valuable volume of translations, *A Book of Russian Verse*. Frances Cornford's translations of *Poems from the Russian* are a remarkable *tour de force*. A volume of translations of the poems of Aragon by her do not fall within the period covered by this essay. These considerable achievements of translation are symptomatic of the interest taken in work abroad by the English poets, which has a most beneficial influence on the work of some young writers. Arthur Waley, whose translations from the Chinese and Japanese were amongst the richest additions to English literature between the two wars, has published no verse translations since 1939, although his prose translation of the Chinese romance, *Monkey*, has the quality of poetry. Other valuable translations from Oriental literature are the *Geeta* and the *Ten Principal Upanishads* translated from the Sanskrit by Shree Purohit Swami, a friend of the late W. B. Yeats. A young Greek poet of great promise, Demetrios Capetanakis, wrote during the war some striking poems in English, poems passionate and spiritual, which those who most admire him believe are likely to have a widening influence as they become better known. Capetanakis, who also wrote criticism, died at an early age.

XII. DYLAN THOMAS, GEORGE BARKER, DAVID GASCOYNE

After Auden and his contemporaries, there was a reaction amongst a slightly younger generation of poets away from a conscious and intellectual style of writing towards the involuntary, the mysterious, the word-intoxicated, the romantic and the Celtic. Of these younger writers, Dylan Thomas is a poet of whom, at times, we can use the word " genius ". He is a master of language

who in his earlier poems at times let language master him.   He
writes in an extremely rhetorical style with a pleasure in the sound
and colour of words which is intoxicating.   He is a "bardic" poet
whose themes are always passionate.   Some of his poems show an
obsession with the imagery of sex and of death.   But he is always
an elemental writer dealing with ideas and images which seem on
the verge of disintegrating into a formless chaos; they are saved by
a simple and grandiose structure and by Thomas's commanding and
picturesque poetic personality.   He is at his best when his poems
are integrated by a single theme, as in a famous poem written before
the war, *In Memory of Ann Jones*.

During the first years of the war, Thomas published little, being
greatly preoccupied by personal matters and, at a later stage, by
various kinds of war work.   Amongst other jobs he did, one was
to write the scripts for documentary films.   In 1943 he began
publishing poems again, in *Horizon* and other magazines.   These
poems are undoubtedly his greatest achievement.   The verboseness
of his early work has disappeared without his sacrificing his rhetorical
power and his love of fine-sounding words.   He uses language with
a power he has never displayed before.   And he has invented new
forms of stanza which are likely to have a lasting influence on the
future of English poetry.

Thomas is a poet who commands the admiration of all contemporary English poets.   He has influenced a number of younger
writers who see in him an alternative to the intellectual writing of
Auden.   Of the poets under forty-five, he is perhaps the only one
capable of exercising a literary influence as great as that of Auden.

During the war, Thomas has written some of his most beautiful
poems, which show a new power of intellectual organisation.   Here
is a poem which seems to me the most beautiful he has written:

Poem in October

It was my thirtieth year to heaven
Woke to my hearing from harbour and neighbour wood
And the mussel pooled and the heron
Priested shore

The morning beckon
With water praying and call of seagull and rock
And the knock of sailing boats on the net-webbed wall
        Myself to set foot
            That second
In the still sleeping town and set forth.

My birthday began with the water—
Birds and the birds of the winged trees flying my name
        Above the farms and the white horses
            And I rose
            In rainy autumn
And walked abroad in a shower of all my days.
High tide and the heron dived when I took the road
            Over the border
            And the gates
Of the town closed as the town awoke.

A springful of larks in a rolling
Cloud and the roadside bushes brimming with whistling
        Blackbirds and the sun of October
            Summery
            On the hill's shoulder,
Here were fond climates and sweet singers suddenly
Come in the morning where I wandered and listened
            To the rain wringing
            Wind blow cold
In the wood faraway under me.

Pale rain over the dwindling harbour
And over the sea-wet church the size of a snail
        With its horns through mist and the castle
            Brown as owls,
            But all the gardens
Of spring and summer were blooming in the tall tales
Beyond the border and under the lark-full cloud.
            There could I marvel
            My birthday
Away but the weather turned around.

It turned away from the blithe country,
And down the other air and the blue altered sky

Streamed again a wonder of summer
With apples
Pears and red currants,
And I saw in the turning so clearly a child's
Forgotten mornings when he walked with his mother
Through the parables
Of sunlight
And the legends of the green chapels.

And the twice told fields of infancy
That his tears burned my cheeks and his heart moved in mine.
These were the woods the river and sea
Where a boy
In the listening
Summertime of the dead whispered the truth of his joy
To the trees and the stones and the fish in the tide.
And the mystery
Sang alive
Still in the water and singing birds.

And there could I marvel my birthday
Away but the weather turned around.   And the true
Joy of the long-dead child sang burning
In the sun
It was my thirtieth
Year to heaven stood there then in the summer noon
Though the town below lay leaved with October blood.
O may my heart's truth
Still be sung
On this high hill in a year's turning.

George Barker is another poet of unreason who is intoxicated with words. But his is a very different case from that of Dylan Thomas. Dylan Thomas strikes me as a master of words. That is to say, although he often writes obscurely and with very little intellectual content in his writing, he handles words with a consummate tact. Although Thomas does not write intellectually, he is obviously a writer of great intellectual force. This cannot be said of Barker, who is essentially a naïf and clumsy writer uncertain of his meanings, hypnotised often with words and ideas which he understands imperfectly, but with a certain visionary power which often compels attention.

During the war Barker has published a volume characteristically and obscurely called *Eros in Dogma*. This volume contains the beautiful sonnet *To My Mother*:

> Most near, most dear, most loved and most far,
> Under the window where I often found her
> Sitting as huge as Asia, seismic with laughter,
> Gin and chicken helpless in her Irish hand,
> Irresistible as Rabelais, but most tender for
> The lame dogs and hurt birds that surround her,—
> She is a procession no one can follow after
> But be like a little dog following a brass band.
>
> She will not glance up at the bomber, or condescend
> To drop her gin and scuttle to a cellar,
> To lean on the mahogany table like a mountain
> Whom only faith can move, and so I send
> O all my faith and all my love to tell her
> That she will move from mourning into morning.

David Gascoyne was in the 1930's the only English surrealist poet of consequence. Recently he has abandoned surrealism and writes limpid poems of personal experience which have the fascination of excerpts from the diary of a sensitive invalid. Gascoyne's poems may well take their place as the most interesting personal record of the mind of a sensitive and intelligent man, written before and during the war. However, they do not only produce an impression of passive suffering. There are also religious poems which create memorable word-pictures, and which reveal a sympathy with the mystical poetry of Pierre Jean Jouve, some of whose poems he has translated. Gascoyne, who has lived in Paris, probably has more in common with his French than with his English fellow poets.

I quote here a passage from *The Gravel-Pit Field*, from the volume *Poems 1937–42*:

> Amidst this nondescript terrain
> Haphazardly the gravel-pit's

WILLIAM EMPSON

KATHLEEN RAINE

Above: MICHAEL ROBERTS, editor of the *Faber Book of Modern Verse* and other collections of the work of the younger poets

Below: M. J. TAMBIMUTTU, editor of *Poetry London*

Above: JOHN LEHMANN, editor of N Writing and Daylight and Penguin N Writing

Below: KEIDRYCH RHYS, editor of *Wales*

Rough-hewn rust-coloured hollows yawn,
Their steep declivities away
From the field-surface dropping down
Towards the depths below where rain-
Water in turbid pools stagnates
Like scraps of sky decaying in
The sockets of a dead man's stare.

The shabby coat of coarse grass spread
Unevenly across the ruts
And humps of lumpy soil; the bits
Of stick and threads of straw; loose clumps
Of weeds with withered stalks and black
Tatters of leaf and scorched pods: all
These intertwined minutiae
Of Nature's humblest growths persist
In their endurance here like rock.

As with untold intensity
On the far edge of Being, where
Life's last faint forms begin to lose
Name and identity and fade
Away into the Void, endures
The final thin triumphant flame
Of all that's most despoiled and bare:
So these least stones, in the extreme
Of their abasement might appear

Like rare stones such as could have formed
A necklet worn by the dead queen
Of a great Pharaoh, in her tomb . . .
So each abandoned snail-shell strewn
Among these blotched dock-leaves might seem
In the pure ray shed by the loss
Of all man-measured value, like
Some priceless pearl-enamelled toy
Cushioned on green silk under glass.

And who in solitude like this
Can say the unclean mongrel's bones
Which stick out, splintered, through the loose

D

Side of a gravel-pit, are not
The precious relics of some saint,
Perhaps miraculous?   Or that
The lettering on this Woodbine-
Packet's remains ought not to read:
Mene mene tekel upharsin?

XIII. POETS WHO HAVE BECOME KNOWN
SINCE 1939

So far I have been writing of poets and poetry which one car
against the background either of a life-time's work, as with 1
Eliot, Edith Sitwell, Edmund Blunden, or else in relation
tendency in literature and to quite recent events which are ne
theless now historic in that they took place in the last decad
with W. H. Auden, Cecil Day Lewis and Louis MacNeice.

Now inevitably I can do little more than point to a few po
of outstanding achievement by writers who have written little,
as Roy Fuller and Henry Reed ; to a few outstanding writers w
it is difficult to relate to any tendency and who, at the same ti
although they have written a striking volume or more, seem to I
exercised little influence on other writers, such as Laurie Lee, F
Prince and Vernon Watkins; and to one or two writers who
vaguely connected with literary movements which have attra
some attention but little result, such as Henry Treece and
Apocalyptics.

Perhaps the most considerable of the poets who appeared s
the war is Vernon Watkins, who like Dylan Thomas is a Welshn
Watkins has been writing for many years, but he did not pul
his first volume until 1941, and this book, *Ballad of the Mari L*
is the result of a great devotion to poetry over many years.   H
a pure poet, devoted only to poetry, inhabiting a world of poe
In this he reminds me of Walter de la Mare, though the influe
most noticeable in his work is W. B. Yeats.   All the value

Watkins' work are poetic ones; his poems produce the impression
of changing the world of experience into beauty and permanence.
In this his work is different from Eliot's search of experience outside time for a religious reason, and Auden's use of poetic symbolism to reconcile psychology, politics and religion in a philosophic
formula.

The first lines of *The Sunbather* illustrate the transmuting method
of Watkins:

> Inert he lies on the saltgold sand
> And sees through his lids the scarlet sky.
> The sea will run back if he breathes a sigh.
> He can hide the sun with a roselit hand.
>
> Loitering, he crossed the single shore
> Where his eyes looked back at the glint of shells.
> With a quoit of stone he startled the bells
> That sleep in the rocks' vibrating core.
>
> Thought-blind to the chosen place he passed.
> The seagulls rose, and circled, and dropped,
> And there, throwing down his coat, he stopped,
> He, touching the mould of the world, lies fast.
>
> The noon-sun dodges around his knee.
> The sand at his head now trembles pale.
> The wind at his temples carries a tale
> And before him flies the bewildered sea.

Vernon Watkins's poems are flights from the real immediately
into the poetic. Some critics would say that such an achievement
of " pure poetry ", an experience which eludes definition, is the
aim of poetry. Nevertheless, the customary use of poetry by most
poets is as a language of symbols and music where transformed
experiences are fused with a philosophy of life which may be
religious or social or personal.

A poet of great charm is Laurie Lee, whose *The Sun My Monument*
was published in 1944. Laurie Lee has not the great technical
versatility nor the developed poetic philosophy of Watkins. He is
a naïf, simple writer, some of whose experiences evidently have

an explosive effect in his mind which produces a spontaneous and
immediate poetry:

At Night

I think at night my hands are mad,
for they follow the irritant texture of darkness
continually carving the sad leaf of your mouth
in the thick black bark of sleep.

And my finger-joints are quick with insanity,
springing with lost amazement
through a vast waste of dreams
and forming frames of desire
around the thought of your eyes.

By day, the print of your body
is like a stroke of sun on my hands,
and the choir of your blood
goes chanting incessantly
through the echoing channels of my wrists.

But I am lost in my hut
when the stars are out,
for my palms have a catlike faculty of sight,
and the surface of every minute
is a swinging image of you.

One poet stands out with Vernon Watkins as of importance.
This is F. T. Prince, who is one of the finest young poets now
writing in English.   F. T. Prince published a first volume, *Poems*,
before the war.   Since the war he has written only a few poems,
one of which, *Soldiers Bathing*, is magnificent:

The sea at evening marbles the warm sand,
And on the level beach I watch the movements of a band
Of soldiers who belong to me.   Stripped bare
For bathing in the sea, they shout and laugh in the soft air.

And all is pathos now.   The body that was gross
Rank, ravenous disgusting, in the act and in repose,
Its fever, filth and sweat, its bestial strength
And bestial decay, now washed in shadow, grows at length

Fragile and luminous.   Poor bare forked animal,
Conscious of his desires and needs and flesh that rise and fall,
Stands in the cool air tasting after toil
The sweetness of his nakedness and lets the sea-waves coil
Their frothy tongues about his feet: forgets
Fear, fear of the war, its terrible pressure that begets
A machinery of death and slavery,
Each being a slave and making slaves of others: finds that he
Remembers lovely freedom in a game,
Mocking himself, and comically mimics fear and shame.

He plays with death and animality:
And reading in the shadows on his pallid flesh I see
The idea of Michelangelo's cartoon
Of soldiers bathing, interrupted before they were half done
By some sortie of the enemy, an episode
Of the Pisan wars with Florence.   I remember how he showed
Their powerful limbs that clambered from the water,
Heads turned across their muscular shoulders, burning for the slaughter,
Forgetful of their bodies that are bare
And eager but to buckle on their weapons lying there.

And I think then of the theme another found
When, shadowing men's bodies on a sinister red ground,
A Florentine, Uccello or Pollaiuolo,
Painted a naked battle.   Warriors, straddled, hacked the foe,
Dug their fierce toes into the soil and slew
Their brother-naked man who lay between their feet and drew
His lips back from his teeth in a grimace.
They were Italians who know war's sorrow and disgrace
And showed the thing suspended, stripped: a theme
Born out of the experience of that horrible extreme
Beneath a sky where even the air flows
With *lachrymae Christi*.   And that rage, that bitterness, those blows,
That hatred of the slain, what could it be
But indirectly or directly a commentary
On the Crucifixion?   So the picture burns
With indignation and pity and despair by turns
Because it is the obverse of that scene
Where Christ hangs murdered, stripped, upon the Cross.   I mean,
That is the explanation of its rage.

And we too have our bitterness and pity that engage
Blood, spirit in this war. But night begins,
Night of the mind: who nowadays is conscious of our sins?
Though every human deed concerns our blood,
And even we must know what nobody had understood,
That some great love is over all we do,
And that is what has driven us to this fury, since so few
Can suffer all the terror of that love:
The terror of that love has set us spinning in this groove
Greased with our blood.

               These wring and dry their hair,
Resume their shirts, forget the fear and shame of being bare:
Because to love is terrible we prefer
The freedom of our crimes. Yet as I drink the dusky air,
I touch a strange delight that fills me full,
Strange gratitude, as if evil itself were beautiful;
And feel the wound of love, while in the west
I see a streak of red that might have issued from Christ's breast.

Henry Reed's first volume, *A Map of Verona*, contains a mysterious and nostalgic poem of great beauty called *Verona*, a soldier's poem of memorable bitterness, *The Naming of Parts*, and contemplative poems on classical and mediaeval themes. When Henry Reed's volume is published he will take his place with F. T. Prince, Vernon Watkins and Terence Tiller as one of the really significant younger poets. A short poem, *The Door and the Window*, gives something of his quality:

My love, you are timely come, let me lie by your heart.
For waking in the dark this morning, I woke to that mystery,
Which we can all wake to, at some dark time or another:
Waking to find the room not as I thought it was,
But the window further away, and the door in another direction.

This was not home, and you were far away,
And I woke sick, and held by another passion,
In the icy grip of a dead, tormenting flame,
Consumed by the night, watched by the door and the window,
On a bed of stone, waiting for the day to bring you.

The window is sunlit now, the spring day sparkles beyond it,
The door has opened: and can you, at last beside me,
Drive under the day that frozen and faithless darkness,
With its unseen torments flickering, which neither
The dearest look nor the longest kiss assuages?

The anthologies of *Poems from the Forces* remind one how many
ts of promise have been killed.   Of these, the most promising
  perhaps Sidney Keyes, who published two volumes, *The Iron
rel* and *The Cruel Solstice*.   The second of these is overshadowed
the sense of his own and others' deaths:

Office for Noon

At the field's border, where the cricket chafes
His brittle wings among the yellow weed,
I pause to hear the sea unendingly sifted
Between the granite fingers of the cape.
At this twelfth hour of unrelenting summer
I think of those whose ready mouths are stopped,
I remember those who crouch in narrow graves,
I weep for those whose eyes are full of sand.

Alun Lewis, also killed, had a real and facile talent.   He wrote
ms and short stories.   He himself thought that his true talent
in prose rather than in verse.
Two young poets of promise are Terence Tiller and G. S.
ser.   Both of these poets share the tendency which seems
ost inevitably associated with the Universities of Oxford and
nbridge.   They are clear, transparent, intellectual poets writing
m their heads rather than from their hearts or their bodies,
lysing their passions and conscious of many difficulties in pro-
ms of sex and life.   Their obscurity, unlike that of the poets
o are followers of Dylan Thomas, comes from a too great intel-
tualisation, a too minute pursuit of their own sensitive reactions,
ir own inner complication and subtle ideas.   Both of them write
disciplined clear poetry in a good, if somewhat invertebrate
dition.   They write lines which give the pleasure of intelligence
nbined with sensibility achieving an effect none the less satis-

factory for its being reliable.   In fact, they are excellent craftsmen.
Here are examples, the first from G. S. Fraser, the second from
Terence Tiller.

> (1) [Fraser] Sometimes the passing walker was the echo
>   Of one who waits on other shores for me,
>   Sometimes the sliding mask of the felucca
>   Spoke of enchanted summer voyages
>   Through rhododendrons or past shining bathers
>   To all my lost imaginary Venuses.

> (2) [Tiller] The sea is beating on the stairs;
>   the room is wise with limbs; hers
>   clutch me with hands of candle-light.
>   And the webbed eyes of love are sweet ;
>   and the soft lath of woman bears
>   a heaven's agonizing weight.

Keidrych Rhys, another Welshman (*The Van Pool*), is a very dis-
organised creative writer, but he has great power at moments.
Alan Rook (*Soldiers, This Solitude*) wrote one of the best poems of
the war in *Dunkirk*.   I should mention also two academic poets of
achievement, Christopher Hassall and Lawrence Whistler.   Alex.
Comfort has written some poems of great clarity and beautiful
imagery in *Elegies*, but it seems likely that his real talent lies in the
direction of prose.   John Heath-Stubbs is a classically-inclined
young poet who has done excellent translations of Leopardi.

If one reads the numerous and significant reviews such as
Horizon, Life and Letters, New Writing, Transformation, Poetry Quarterly
and *Poetry London* in which the young writers write, one has the
impression that the young writers are concerned with other things
than the ideology of British Democracy, and that while they tend
to support the policy of the Left, it does not command their enthusiasm.   They have abandoned the hope of an integration of their
own highest interests, their own humanity, their own personalities within any politically organised society.   In this, they have
reacted sharply from the writers of the 1930's.   They are concerned partly with trying to construct a vision of the time which

accepts the fact of social disintegration, partly with trying to develop their own taste and talent within their own isolated conspiracy of intelligent and frustrated minds.   During the war, the work of poets of the Forces nearly always reflected the terrible experience of war, and scarcely looked beyond that experience.   A singular and powerful poem by a young member of the Fleet Air Arm, Roy Fuller, sums up exactly the view of his generation.   Here are the first four stanzas of this poem, *What is Terrible*, of eight stanzas, published in *A Lost Season*:

> Life at last I know is terrible:
> The innocent scene, the innocent walls and light
> And hills for me are like the cavities
> Of surgery or dreams.   The visible might
> Vanish, for all it reassures, in white.
>
> This apprehension has come slowly to me
> Like symptoms and bulletins of sickness.   I
> Must first be moved across two oceans, then
> Bored, systematically and sickeningly,
> In a place where war is news.   And constantly
>
> I must be threatened with what is certainly worse:
> Peril and death, but no less boring.   And
> What else?   Besides my fear, my misspent time,
> My love, hurt and postponed, there is the hand
> Moving the empty glove; the bland
>
> Aspect of nothing disguised as something; that
> Part of living incommunicable,
> For which we try to find vague adequate
> Images, and which, after all,
> Is quite surprisingly communicable.

Enormous quantities of poems have been produced in war-time Britain, for there has been a boom in poetry and several publishers have been glad to use much of their paper in printing books of it. At first the general impression produced by this poetry has been one of disintegration.   If one compares anthologies such as *Poems from the Forces* and *The White Horseman* with the collection produced by the imagists or any other advanced movement since 1918, one notices at once the lack of rhythmic tension, the confused imagery, the over-literary fashions of thought, the uncritical writing which stakes all its ambition on a vague faith in inspiration or on some preconceived if chaotic attitude towards life.

It is not to the "movements" that I would look for any promising signs in English poetry today, but to poets and to poems. Treece, the leader of the Apocalyptic movement, is a writer of individuality, and perhaps it is not his fault that his greatest weaknesses have been singled out for approval by his admirers. Here he is writing at his best in *Lincolnshire Bomber Station*:

> Across the road the homesick Romans made
> The ground-mist thickens to a milky shroud;
> Through flat, damp fields call sheep, mourning their dead
> In cracked and timeless voices, unutterably sad,
> Suffering for all the world, in Lincolnshire.
>
> And I wonder how the Romans liked it here;
> Flat fields, no sun, the muddy misty dawn,
> And always, above all, the mad rain dripping down,
> Rusting sword and helmet, wetting the feet
> And soaking to the bone, down to the very heart.

Amongst the Apocalyptic writers there appeared, in addition to Henry Treece, G. S. Fraser, J. F. Hendry, Norman McCaig, Nicholas Moore, Vernon Watkins, Tom Scott. Of these, only Treece and Hendry could be said really to have any aims in common. G. S. Fraser is far more in the tradition of the poets whom Oxford and Cambridge Universities have been producing for some years, who write poems recording their immediate reactions to scenery, events and love affairs, in poems that are a young man's letters to his circle of witty and graceful friends.

Nicholas Moore is a poet with a fund of gaiety and bright colour in his writing. He rarely writes with any close concentration and his work produces an impression of a light clear atmosphere in which he can develop ideas freely, rather than with any intensity.

XIV. REGIONALISM

Some readers may have noticed that in this section I have
entioned several young Welsh poets—Vernon Watkins, Keidrych
ays, Alun Lewis.   Regionalism is beginning to become a cultural
ovement (or, rather, several cultural movements) to reckon with,
pecially since Wales, Ireland and Scotland now have some of the
ost original poets writing in the British Isles.

Regionalism counts as a literary movement and not just as
olitics masquerading as poetry or as a propaganda for advertising
rtain cliques, because it contributes to the creation of a virile,
ugh poetic language.   English has become a language misused,
afficked, stretched thin, turned abstract, officialised and castrated
all the uses of Empire, business, newspapers and broadcasting.
e most genuine impulse behind every literary movement in
cent years has been to invent a concrete and human use of this
nguage which in millions of minds all over the world is now no
nger a living tongue but a kind of vast calculating machine.

The idea of reviving local dialects and local uses of speech has
en tried often before and will be tried again.   It is obviously
althy in principle;   the question really is whether the conditions
the modern world, which seems to be feeling its way towards a
orld language, admit the principle of the multiplication of lan-
ages for the sake of literature.

It may well be, though, that European literature is on the point
dividing into two streams, one that of an easily translatable,
ternational literature of general ideas and wide, social emotions;
e other, of a regional, particular literature absorbed in local tradi-
ons and the colour of language in particular places.   The develop-
ent of an international kind of European literature and a regional
erature at the same time is not incompatible;   rather, the two
nds would be complementary to each other.

Several Scottish poets have in recent years taken to writing in
cots, an English strengthened with Scottish idiom, and even in

Gaelic. The most famous of these poets, living today, is Hugh McDiarmid. McDiarmid is evidently a man of dominating personality, capable of writing in a dominating language. His poetry suffers from what appears to be the poet's extreme egotism and intellectual arrogance, which persuades him that form would be an intolerable restraint on the expression of his roving thoughts, all of which seem to him to be of equal interest. Despite these faults, McDiarmid is a powerful and fascinating writer. His long, shapeless poems often contain passages of rugged beauty and ideas expressed with force and clarity.

Adam Drinan is an islander who writes very beautifully of the life of the Scottish islands. W. S. Graham is a follower of Dylan Thomas, but he has an original vein of his own. Ruthven Todd is less intransigeantly a Scot than these others. He is a charming and personal poet. I cannot pretend to enjoy the vast vistas opened up by the poems of J. F. Hendry, who is an Apocalyptic follower of Henry Treece.

An interesting poet of this movement is Francis Scarfe, a Tynesider, who uses an imagery influenced perhaps by Garcia Lorca. His poems have the simplicity and sincerity of an honest and sensitive man.

Douglas Young adds at least six other languages to his Scots in his *Letter to Hugh McDiarmid, 1940*. Norman Nicholson, a native of Cumberland, whose first volume of poems, *Five Rivers*, was awarded the Heinemann prize for 1945, is another regional poet of real talent.

The Welsh writers have a magazine called *Wales* edited by Keidrych Rhys, and the Scottish one called *Poetry Scotland*. Their editorials deplore the literary tendencies of England; most of the authors also appear in English publications, however. These regional writers probably have a genuine grievance that so much of British culture is produced in London and that the writer who happens to live in London gets more attention than the writer in Edinburgh or Cardiff.

If Northern Ireland has not produced a " movement ", it has produced at least two distinguished contemporary poets—Louis

MacNeice, and W. R. Rodgers, a forceful poet with a gift distantly reminiscent of that of another Ulster clergyman (W. R. Rodgers is in Orders), Jonathan Swift.

XV. SUMMING UP

It would be most gratifying to be able to end this essay with some high-sounding claim such as that the present generation of modern English poets is the greatest since the Elizabethans. This would justify the reader in taking the trouble to inquire into the merits of all the poets discussed here. He would be sure that in doing so he was truly in contact with greatness.

But as a critic writing in good faith, it is impossible for me to make any claim. If modern literature existed within a fixed tradition, then it would be possible to judge it by standards of technique and sensibility derived from that tradition. But modern writers are governed by no traditional rules accepted by themselves and their critics. What is meant even by " tradition " is highly disputable, because the strength of a tradition in the arts has a certain relation (though a difficult one to define) to its claims to present a picture of contemporary life. When life changes violently, then the tradition either becomes academic and remote from life, and therefore loses its force and in that sense ceases to be traditional, or else it transforms itself and adapts itself to life, thus preserving the traditional relationship to life (which is the most living and important aspect of a tradition). But a transformed tradition may be almost unrecognisable, if one attempts to judge it by the familiar appearance of past traditional literature. Thus some of the most revolutionary works in modern English, such as T. S. Eliot's *The Waste Land* and James Joyce's *Ulysses* exercise the highest claims to be regarded as traditional. At the same time, these claims are difficult for contemporaries to judge because there are no academic and established standards by which to judge them.

In brief, it is the Future alone which can judge our modern

poetry. The Future alone can make those ruthless simplificati
which we cannot afford to make as we examine each modern po
closely and admire it for that complexity which may be exactly
quality which the Future will refuse to interest itself in, just as
public today finds in the involved metaphorical language of so
seventeenth century poets a reason for disregarding instead of
admiring them.

Yet when we have recognised the limitations of our judgemen
there are still two reasons for recommending the study of mode
English poetry as of the highest interest. One is that after all the
are a dozen or so poets writing today who may indeed be amo
the company of immortal poets. One can certainly submit mu
modern poetry to a minute and exact study and then report th
there are lines in T. S. Eliot, Blunden, Graves, Edith Sitwe
Auden, Dylan Thomas, Empson and MacNeice which seem to co
pare with the great achievements of English poetry. There a
memorable images in all these poets, there is a highly individu
music. The poetic personality of a writer such as Robert Grav
or William Empson, wizened, eccentric, crabbed as it seems
times, appears to have an authentic and permanent interest.

If we should not fall into the trap of making exalted claims, v
should not, either, be too modest. The critics who dismiss th
whole of modern poetry as worthless are rather more likely to
wrong than those who can only interest themselves in it if they a
assured of its greatness and permanence. What one can say ce
tainly is that everywhere in modern English poetry one comes upo
evidence of things truly and sincerely created. Everywhere the
is evidence of a restless mental energy, lively invention, sincerit
of feeling.

The second reason for concerning oneself with modern Englis
poetry arises from the consideration of this mental energy, th
poetic activity of which I have just spoken. Whether or n
modern poetry is " great ", the poets nevertheless are in some sens
representatives of the poetic sensibility of our past and very grea
tradition. They are men and women who have read poetry an
who have associated with the minds of past poets. If we valu

poetry at all, we know that no question would be of more interest to answer than " What would Shakespeare or Dante or Racine say of our age if he were living today ? " No cry in poetry is more heartfelt than Wordsworth's: " Milton, thou should'st be living at this hour, England hath need of thee ! " And to a certain extent this cry was purely rhetorical for in a sense the poet who uttered it himself represented the spirit of Milton.

It is possible that the greatest poets are to some extent the fortunate products of their time. Shakespeare born fifty years later, or born in our own time, would not have been the Shakespeare we know. Born today, he might well have been a lesser poet: yet we might well feel that the benefit of a Shakespearean sensibility amongst us today would in certain ways be more valuable than the whole of Shakespeare's work written four hundred years ago. There is a sense in which modern painting or modern poetry, quite apart from all questions of its intrinsic greatness, is worth more to us than all the painting and literature of the past, because it is the world of our own eyes seen through the eyes of the representatives of a great tradition.

The question, therefore, to ask ourselves is not whether our modern poets are among the giants of the poetry of all time, but whether, while being faithful, as far as we can judge, to the greatest traditions of poetry, they also, with all their power and sensibility live amongst us and interpret our world in the light of that tradition. " Milton, thou should'st be living at this hour ! " " Be Milton ! Be Shakespeare ! to the best of your capacity ! " is the message of Virginia Woolf in her *Letter to a Young Poet*.

What we can surely claim is that our poets do provide this unique contribution of creating a poetry which is not merely an imitation of the past, but which is " modern ", which does therefore have a value for us which the greatest poets might have, if, transformed, they were living amongst us today, applying themselves to our world and our problems. Modern English poetry is alive. It may be struggling through darkness towards the light. It may be that future generations will reject nine-tenths of it. But that does not prevent its being of the greatest interest to us, because it provides us with the invaluable experience of the poetic sensibility of all times—past and future—adapting itself to *our* conditions, *our* suffering, *our* struggle. And if the Future is not interested in our poets, it will not be interested in us either. But we are, inevitably, and rightly, interested in ourselves.

Above: ALUN LEWIS   *Above*: SYDNEY KEYES
Below: F. T. PRINCE   *Below*: JOHN HEATH STUBBS

Above: HENRY TREECE
Below: ROY FULLER

Above: ALEX. COMFORT
Below: LAURIE LEE

SELECT BIBLIOGRAPHY

Compiled by W. M.

W. H. AUDEN—*Poems* (1930); *The Orators* (1932); *The Dance of Death* (1933); *Look Stranger* (1936); *Another Time* (1940); *New Year Letter* (1941); *For the Time Being* (1945).

Poetic Drama—*The Dog Beneath the Skin* (1935); *The Ascent of F 6* (1936) (with Christopher Isherwood).

Prose—*Journey to a War* (1939) (with Christopher Isherwood); *Letters from Iceland* (1941) (with Louis MacNeice).

GEORGE BARKER—*Alanna Autumnal* (1933); *Poems* (1935); *Janus* (1935); *Calamiterror* (1937); *Lament and Triumph* (1940); *Eros in Dogma* (1944).

JOHN BETJEMAN—*Continual Dew* (1937); *Old Lights for New Chancels* (1940); *New Bats in Old Belfries* (1945).

Edited (with G. Taylor): *English, Scottish and Welsh Landscape Verse 1700–1860* (1944).

Prose—*Ghastly Good Taste* (1933); *An Oxford University Chest* (1938); *Antiquarian Prejudice* (1939).

LAURENCE BINYON (1869–1942)—*Collected Poems* (1931); *The North Star, and Other Poems* (1941); *The Burning of the Leaves* (1944).

Already famous as a poet during the First World War, and author of many books on European and Oriental art. Verse translations of Dante's Purgatorio, Inferno, and Paradiso, the last completed shortly before the poet's death.

EDMUND BLUNDEN—*Poems 1914–30* (1935); *Poems 1930–40* (1941).

Prose—*On the Poems of Henry Vaughan* (1927); *Undertones of War* (1928); *Nature in English Literature* (1929); *Leigh Hunt* (1930); *The Face of England* (1932); *Charles Lamb and his Contemporaries* (1934); *The Mind's Eye* (1934); *Keats' Publisher* (1936); *English Villages* (1941); *Thomas Hardy* (1942); *Cricket Country* (1944); *Shelley* (1946); etc.

GORDON BOTTOMLEY—*Poems of Thirty Years* (1925)

Drama—*King Lear's Wife and other Plays* (1920); *Lyric Plays* (1932); *The Acts of St. Peter* (1933); *Choric Plays* (1939); *Deirdire* (in English and Gaelic) (1944); *Kate Kennedy* (1945); etc.

RONALD BOTTRALL—*The Loosening and Other Poems* (1931); *Festivals of Fire* (1934); *The Turning Path* (1939); *Farewell and Welcome* (1945).

LILIAN BOWES LYON—*Bright Feather Fading* (1936); *Evening in Stepney* (1943).

NORMAN CAMERON—*The Winter House* (1935). Translated: *Selected Verse Poems of Arthur Rimbaud* (1942).

DEMETRIOS CAPETANAKIS—He has published most frequently in *New Writing*. A collection of his poetry and prose has appeared under the title: *Demetrios Capetanakis; A Greek Poet in England*.

ALEX. COMFORT—*A Wreath for the Living* (1942); *Elegies* (1944).
Novels—*The Almond Tree* (1943); *The Power House* (1944).

CECIL DAY LEWIS—*Collected Poems 1929–33* (1935); *A Time to Dance* (1935); *Overtures to Death* (1938); *The Georgics of Virgil* (a verse translation) (1940); *Word Over All* (1943).
Novels—*The Friendly Tree* (1936); *Starting Point* (1937); *The Echoing Green* (1938); *Child of Misfortune* (1939).
Criticism—*A Hope for Poetry* (1934); *Poetry for You* (1945).

WALTER DE LA MARE—*Poems* (1906); *The Listeners and Other Poems* (1912); *Peacock Pie* (1913); *Motley and Other Poems* (1918); *The Veil and Other Poems* (1921); *The Fleeting and Other Poems* (1933); *Memory and Other Poems* (1938); *Bells and Grass* (1941); *Collected Poems* (1942); *Collected Rhymes and Verses* (1944); *The Burning Glass and Other Poems* (1945).
Anthologies (with very full commentaries)—*Come Hither* (1923); *Early One Morning* (1935); *Behold This Dreamer!* (1939); *Love* (1943).
Prose—*Henry Brocken* (1904); *The Return* (1910); *Memoirs of a Midget* (1921); *The Riddle and Other Stories* (1923); *The Three Mulla-Mulgars* (1924); *Broomsticks and Other Tales* (1925); *The Connoisseur and Other Stories* (1926); *The Lord Fish and Other Stories* (1933); *The Magic Jacket and Other Stories* (1943); *The Scarecrow and Other Stories* (1944); etc.

ADAM DRINAN—*The Men of the Rocks* (1942); *The Ghosts of the Strath* (1943); *Women of the Happy Island* (1945).

LAWRENCE DURRELL—*A Private Country* (1943); *Cities, Plains and People* (1946).
Novel—*The Black Book* (1938).

T. S. ELIOT—*Collected Poems 1909–1935* (1936); *East Coker* (1940); *Burnt Norton* (1941); *The Dry Salvages* (1941); *Little Gidding* (1942); the last four published together as *Four Quartets* (1944).

Poetic Drama—*The Rock* (1934); *Murder in the Cathedral* (1935); *The Family Reunion* (1939).

Prose—*Sacred Wood* (1920); *The Use of Poetry and the Use of Criticism* (1933); *After Strange Gods* (1934); *Elizabethan Essays* (1934); *The Idea of a Christian Society* (1939); *What is a Classic?* (1945); etc.

WILLIAM EMPSON—*Poems* (1935); *The Gathering Storm* (1940).

Prose—*Seven Types of Ambiguity* (1930); *Some Versions of the Pastoral* (1935).

G. S. FRASER—*The Fatal Landscape* (1941); *Home Town Elegy* (1944).

ROY FULLER—*The Middle of a War* (1942); *A Lost Season* (1944).

DAVID GASCOYNE—*Man's Life is this Meat* (1934); *Poems 1937–42* (1943).

Prose—*A Short Survey of Surrealism* (1935); *Holderlin's Madness* (1938).

W. S. GRAHAM—*Cage Without Grievance* (1943); *The Seven Journeys* (1944); *Second Poems* (1945).

ROBERT GRAVES—*Collected Poems* (1938); *No More Ghosts* (selected poems) (1940); *Poems 1938–45* (1945).

Novels—*I, Claudius* (1934); *Claudius the God* (1934); *Count Belisarius* (1938); *Sergeant Lamb of the Ninth* (1940); *Proceed, Sergeant Lamb* (1941); *Wife to Mr. Milton* (1943); *The Golden Fleece* (1944); etc.

GEOFFREY GRIGSON (Editor of *New Verse*)—*Several Observations* (1939); *Under the Cliff and Other Poems* (1943).

Edited: *New Verse* (anthology) (1940); *The Poet's Eye* (1944).

CHRISTOPHER HASSALL—*Poems of Two Years* (1935); *Devil's Dyke* (1936); *Christ's Comet* (1937); *Penthesperon* (1938); *Crisis* (1939); *S.O.S.—Ludlow* (1940).

JOHN HEATH-STUBBS—*Wounded Thammuz* (1942); *Beauty and the Beast* (1944).

J. F. HENDRY—*The Bombed Happiness* (1942); *The Orchestral Mountain* (1943).

Contributions to *The White Horseman* (with Nicholas Moore, G. S. Fraser, Tom Scott, Henry Treece, Vernon Watkins and other writers of the New Apocalypse movement) (1941).

SIDNEY KEYES—*The Iron Laurel* (1942); *The Cruel Solstice* (1944); *Collected Poems* (1945).

LAURIE LEE—*The Sun My Monument* (1944).

JOHN LEHMANN (Editor of *New Writing and Daylight* and *Penguin New Writing*)—*The Sphere of Glass* (1944).
Prose—*A Garden Revisited* (1931); *The Noise of History* (1934); *Prometheus and the Bolsheviks* (1937); *Evil was Abroad* (1938); *Down River* (1939); *New Writing in Europe* (1940).

ALUN LEWIS—*Raiders' Dawn* (1942); *Ha! Ha! Among the Trumpets* (1945).
Prose—*The Last Inspection* (short stories) (1942).

NORMAN MCCAIG—*Far Cry* (1943).

"HUGH MCDIARMID" (C. M. Grieve) (Editor of *The Voice of Scotland*)—*Sangschaw*; *Penny Wheep*; *A Drunk Man looks at the Thistle*; *To Circumjack Cencrastus*; *Stony Limits and other Poems*; *First Hymn to Lenin*; *Second Hymn to Lenin*; *Cornish Heroic Song for Valda Trevlyn*; *Selected Poems* (1945).
Edited: *Golden Treasury of Scottish Poetry*.
Prose—*Scottish Scene* (1934); *At the Sign of the Thistle* (1934); *Lucky Poet* (autobiography) (1943), etc.

LOUIS MACNEICE—*Poems* (1935); *The Agamemnon of Aeschylus* (translation) (1936); *Out of the Picture* (1937); *The Earth Compels* (1938); *Autumn Journal* (1939); *Plant and Phantom* (1941); *Springboard* (1944).
Prose—*I Crossed the Minch* (1939); *Letters from Iceland* (with W. H. Auden) (1941).

CHARLES MADGE—*The Disappearing Castle* (1937); *The Father Found* (1941).

FRED MARNAU—*The Wounds of the Apostles* (1944).

NICHOLAS MOORE—*The Glass Tower* (1945).

EDWIN MUIR—*First Poems* (1925); *Chorus of the Newly Dead* (1926); *Six Poems* (1932); *Variations on a Time Theme* (1934); *Journeys and Places* (1937); *The Narrow Place* (1943).
Translations (with Willa Muir)—Hermann Broch's *The Sleepwalkers* (1932); Franz Kafka's *The Trial* (1937).
Prose—*Transition* (criticism) (1926); *The Structure of the Novel* (1928); *John Knox* (1929); *Scottish Journey* (1935); *Scott and Scotland* (1936); *The Story and the Fable* (autobiography) (1940).
Novels—*The Marionette* (1927); *The Three Brothers* (1931); *Poor Tom* (1932).

Norman Nicholson—*Five Rivers* (1944); *The Old Man of the Mountains* (poetic drama) (1946).
  Edited: *An Anthology of Religious Verse* (1942).
  Prose—*Man and Literature* (1943).

Ruth Pitter—*First Poems* (1920); *First and Second Poems* (1927); *A Mad Lady's Garland* (1934); *A Trophy of Arms* (1936); *The Spirit Watches* (1939); *The Rude Potato* (humorous verse) (1941); *The Bridge* (1945).

F. T. Prince—*Poems* (1938).

Kathleen Raine—*Stone and Flower* (1943).
  Translation—Denis de Rougemont's *Talk of the Devil*.

Herbert Read—*Poems 1914–34* (1935); *Thirty-five Poems* (1940); *A World Within a War* (1944).
  Prose—*In Retreat* (1925); *Reason and Romanticism* (1928); *English Prose Style* (1928); *Phases of English Poetry* (1928); *The Sense of Glory* (1929); *Wordsworth* (1930); *The Meaning of Art* (1931); *Form in Modern Poetry* (1932); *The Innocent Eye* (1933); *Art Now* (1933); *The Green Child* (1935); *In Defence of Shelley* (1935); *Art and Society* (1936); *Poetry and Anarchism* (collected essays) (1938); *Annals of Innocence and Experience* (autobiography) (1940); *The Politics of the Unpolitical* (1943); *Education Through Art* (1943); etc.

Henry Reed—*A Map of Verona* (1946); has published in *New Writing, The New Statesman, The Listener*, etc.

Keidrych Rhys (Editor of *Wales*)—*The Van Pool, and Other Poems* (1942).
  Edited: *Poems from the Forces* (1942); *More Poems from the Forces* (1943).

Anne Ridler—*The Nine Bright Shiners* (1943); *Cain* (a verse lay) (1944).
  Edited: *A Little Book of Modern Verse* (1942).

Michael Roberts—*Poems* (1936); *Orion Marches* (1939).
  Edited: *New Signatures* (1932); *The Faber Book of Modern Verse* (1936); *The Faber Book of Comic Verse* (1942).
  Prose—*Critique of Poetry* (1934); *The Modern Mind* (1937); *T. E. Hulme* (1938); *The Recovery of the West* (1941).

Alan Rook—*Soldiers, This Solitude* (1942); *These are My Comrades* (1943).

Siegfried Sassoon—*Counter Attack* (1918); *Satirical Poems* (1926); *The Heart's Journey* (1928); *Vigils* (1935); *Rhymed Ruminations* (1940); etc.

Prose—*Memoirs of a Foxhunting Man* (1928); *Memoirs of an Infantry Officer* (1930); *Sherston's Progress* (1936); *The Old Century* (1938); *The Weald of Youth* (1942); *Siegfried's Journey* (1945).

FRANCIS SCARFE—*Inscapes* (1940); *Forty Poems and Ballads* (1941).
Criticism—*Auden and After: the Liberation of Poetry* (1942).

TOM SCOTT—No book; has published with the New Apocalypse group in *The White Horseman,* etc.

E. J. SCOVELL—*Shadows of Chrysanthemums* (1944).

EDITH SITWELL—*Collected Poems* (1930); *Street Songs* (1942); *Green Song* (1944); *The Song of the Cold* (1945).

Prose—*Alexander Pope* (1930); *Bath* (1932); *The English Eccentrics* (1933); *Aspects of Modern Poetry* (1934); *Victoria of England* (1936). Edited: *The Pleasures of Poetry* (anthology) (1931).

STEPHEN SPENDER—*Twenty Poems* (1930); *Poems* (Vienna, 1936); *Trial of a Judge* (verse drama) (1938); *Poems from Spain* (1939); *The Still Centre* (1939); *Ruins and Visions* (1942); *Poems of Dedication* (1946). Prose—*The Destructive Element* (criticism) (1936); *Forward from Liberalism* (1937); *The Backward Son* (novel) (1940); *Citizens in War —and After* (the civil defence services) (1945); *Life and the Poet* (1942); *European Witness* (1946).

JULIAN SYMONS—*Confusion about X* (1939); *The Second Man* (1944). Edited: *An Anthology of War Poetry* (1943).

M. J. TAMBIMUTTU (Editor of *Poetry London*)—Edited: *Poetry in Wartime* (1942).

DYLAN THOMAS—*25 Poems* (1936); *The Map of Love: Verse and Prose* (1939); *18 Poems* (1942); *Deaths and Entrances* (1945).

TERENCE TILLER—*Selected Poems* (1941); *The Inward Animal* (1944).

RUTHVEN TODD—*Until Now* (1942); *The Planet in My Hand* (1945); *Acreage of the Heart* (1945).
Novel—*The Lost Traveller* (1944).
Edited: Gilchrist's *Life of William Blake* (1942).

HENRY TREECE—*Thirty-eight Poems* (1940); *Invitation and Warning* (1942); *The Black Seasons* (1945).

British Book News, *a monthly classified and annotated selection of books on all subjects, can be obtained free by residents outside Britain on application to the* National Book League, 7 Albemarle Street, London, W.1.

PROSE LITERATURE SINCE 1939

This short critical survey of English prose writing from 1939 to 1945 is intended to give those readers who are interested in contemporary English Literature an account of the most important work published during the war years. It covers all kinds of prose writing, critical, biographical, or descriptive, whose interest is more than transient. Novels and short stories are not included, but form the subject of another of the essays in this series.

Mr. John Hayward is distinguished both as scholar and critic. He was born in 1905 and is a graduate of King's College, Cambridge. He returned to Cambridge at the beginning of the war, and from there wrote regularly for the Ministry of Information on current books. Before the war he was for a time the London literary correspondent of the *New York Sun*, and has been for several years the contributor of a "London Letter" to the Swedish literary periodical *Bonniers Litterära Magasin*. Among his published works are editions of Rochester, Donne, Swift, and St. Evremont ; a number of anthologies, including selections of 19th Century Poetry, and 17th Century Poetry ; and a biography of Charles II. He has over a long period reviewed for the *Criterion*, *The Times Literary Supplement*, and other leading papers, is an expert on bibliography, and an editorial adviser to a London publisher.

Total War: The Heart of a City

PROSE LITERATURE
SINCE 1939

By

JOHN HAYWARD

Illustrated

Published for
THE BRITISH COUNCIL
by LONGMANS GREEN & CO
LONDON   NEW YORK   TORONTO

LONGMANS, GREEN AND CO. LTD.
OF PATERNOSTER ROW
43 ALBERT DRIVE, LONDON, S.W.19
NICOL ROAD, BOMBAY
17 CHITTARANJAN AVENUE, CALCUTTA
36A MOUNT ROAD, MADRAS

LONGMANS, GREEN AND CO.
55 FIFTH AVENUE, NEW YORK, 3

LONGMANS, GREEN AND CO.
215 VICTORIA STREET, TORONTO, 1

LONGMANS' CODE NUMBER: 10037

THIS BOOKLET IS PRODUCED IN
COMPLETE CONFORMITY WITH THE
AUTHORISED ECONOMY STANDARDS

C

BRITISH COUNCIL'S CODE NAME: PROSE (ENGLISH)

First published 1947

SET IN MONOTYPE PERPETUA
DESIGNED BY ERIC GILL

PRINTED IN GREAT BRITAIN
BY R. & R. CLARK, LIMITED, EDINBURGH

CONTENTS

ILLUSTRATIONS

The opinions expressed in this book are the author's,
and not necessarily those of the British Council

PROSE LITERATURE SINCE 1939

A SURVEY OF ENGLISH PROSE LITERATURE
OTHER THAN FICTION FROM 1939 TO 1945

I. INTRODUCTION

THE purpose of this essay is, briefly, to give readers outside the British Isles a tentative account of the achievement of English prose literature (other than fiction) during the five years of war from 1939 to 1945. An attempt to do more than this would be premature. It is still too early to see those years in perspective; and until this is possible no final literary judgements can be passed. Even in peace-time it would be difficult and scarcely profitable to trace so soon and through such a limited and arbitrary period, those currents and cross-currents of contemporary thought and sensibility which condition a writer's work. Indeed, if Britain had been at peace during those years, there would be little point in treating them as a "special" literary period; and an interim statement of this nature would be uncalled-for. But, during those five years, Britain was involved in the greatest crisis in her history; and during part of them in a desperate and lonely struggle for mere survival. For five years, the energies, mental and spiritual no less than physical, of the whole nation were conscripted for one end; and the activities and interests of every man and woman were directed, if not actually prescribed, by the over-riding needs of the State.

Under conditions of total war, literary activity, like any other, is compelled more or less to serve the interest of the community. It is not only that restrictions are applied in the interests of national security; that both the expression of ideas and the statement of facts are liable to be censored or discouraged; that the raw material of books and the means for their production and distribution are inevitably limited by their diversion to more urgent purposes; and that large numbers of those engaged in the creation of books— writers, publishers, compositors, binders, and booksellers—are called away to serve with the armed forces or in the enormously expanded departments of the central government. It is not only in these respects that literature becomes involved in the waging of total war. The entire aspect of the human situation is altered by the violent distortions of society in war-time. The disruption of domestic life; the hardship caused by evacuation, requisitioning of houses, and the absence of the breadwinner; the reorganisation of industry and commerce for war production and transport; the problems of displaced labour and long hours; the boredom of monotonous diet and inadequate recreation; the depression of the black-out, and the strain of air-raids, actual or anticipated—are all instruments of this change. The climate of thought and sensibility must be profoundly affected by such disturbances in the conventional and accepted order of things.

In the exacting circumstances and inhibiting conditions of the years 1939–1945, it is not so much surprising that books were written and published as that any were written at all. In fact, a great many were written and published, though fewer in number and in far smaller editions than the public was eager to buy. Its craving for books was doubtless stimulated by the close confinement in which most people were forced to live; by lack of other forms of entertainment; and by the prolonged satisfaction a book can give compared with the brief enjoyment of a film or radio programme. But this craving, though largely adventitious, was still the expression of a real need for spiritual refreshment, mental exercise, and emotional relief. The publishers did their best to satisfy it. They fought successfully to prevent the imposition of a purchase-tax on books; they fought incessantly, though with small success, for an increase in their basic paper ration—a bare 40 per cent of the less than average amount used in 1938–1939—and, failing, made the best use of what they were allowed by conforming to certain standards of economy, which regrettably, but inevitably, lowered the prestige of British book-production. Their most difficult problem was, however, to balance fairly the claims on their resources of new books and reprints. The demand for the classics of English literature was unprecedented throughout the war and was never near being satisfied, for the simple reason that no publisher could afford to jeopardise his goodwill and his future by neglecting the living writer in favour of the dead. The publishers of such well-known collections as "Everyman" and "The World's Classics" endeavoured to keep as many titles in print as they could, and their efforts were supplemented by supplies of the wonderfully cheap "Penguin" reprints, which even the fastidious reader very soon learned not to despise. Yet, long after the end of the war, it was still almost impossible to buy a new copy of a novel, for example, by Jane Austen or Anthony Trollope. Established living authors, especially those in the class of "best-sellers", were naturally given more consideration than a publisher could risk giving to an untried and unknown writer. Even so, the supply of freshly reprinted copies of the works of contemporary authors never kept pace with the demand, and some of the most illustrious of them suffered in their reputations as well as in their pockets—an economic fact which should not be under-estimated by the literary historian— from their books being forced out of print for months and even a year or more at a time. The novice suffered worst, simply because most publishers were too deeply committed to launch a new writer at the expense of their other obligations. That some new writers, at least, were given a chance to make a name for themselves, in spite of such competition, must be counted to the credit of those publishers whose faith in the continuity of English literature, unshaken by the temptation to make easy and immediate profits from reprints, was strong enough to allow the allocation of paper and labour to this commendable end.

It must be recorded, in passing, that many self-styled publishers set up in business during the war. Profiting by the anomaly that only those publishers who were in business before the war were subject to the restrictions of the Paper Controller, they were free to acquire what parcels of loose paper they could from jobbing printers and other odd sources. With no established connections, with no stock-in-trade to replace or enlarge, it might be supposed that they would have taken advantage of their position to sponsor new talent. Instead, they were in the main content to print or reprint any trash that would sell to the semi-illiterate reader at a maximum profit and minimum cost of production. They specialised in particular in cheap children's books, cunningly marketed as substitutes for those gifts which even in war-time children expect and grown-ups cannot deny. Their activities would not be worth mentioning but for the fact that they wasted paper which more responsible publishers badly needed and would have used for worthier purposes. The volume of their paltry productions, though it swelled the total number of books published during the war, would give anyone not aware of these facts a false impression of the literary activity of those years.

It has been pointed out that the scarcity of paper and labour (notably in the binding trade) was prejudicial to new writers. It is hardly necessary to add that if relatively few new names appeared in the publishers' lists between 1939 and 1945, this was due as much, if not more, to the fact that potential young writers of both sexes were conscripted for national service and had little chance of pursuing a literary career, except spasmodically and against extra-ordinary hindrances. Certainly those who succeeded somehow in putting pen to paper could not reasonably be expected to have either the time or the resources to make any extended contribution to prose literature. Their modest and occasional efforts tended to take the form of lyrics, short stories, and incidental reporting of current events, and were published in magazines and anthologies, notably in *Horizon*, *Penguin New Writing*, and *Poetry (London)*.

If the exigencies of the times were almost wholly unfavourable to the young and unrecognised writers, they were hardly less so to the experienced and established. It is indeed remarkable that the latter managed to do any literary work at all in addition to their war service. For, throughout the war, men and women were liable to conscription up to the age of fifty-one, and Home Guard duty, fire-watching, arduous domestic tasks, and voluntary service of many kinds occupied the great majority of those who were not conscripted or were above this age-limit. In particular, it is necessary for a proper understanding of the literary situation during the war to know that many writers and intellectuals of acknowledged ability were directed into jobs in which their special talents could be profitably used for the prosecution of the war. This is an important fact. For, though such work does in a sense keep a writer in training, it is by its nature and the excessive pressure under which it is done more likely than not to exhaust his capacity for thought and composition and so drain away any desire to write, not for a living since that is secured to him officially, but for pleasure. It would be interesting, but unnecessary here to quote the names of the large number—a high proportion in fact—of more or less well-known authors, critics, reviewers, and teachers, of both sexes, whose literary abilities were enlisted for such services as propaganda, intelligence, research, information, broadcasting, and planning.

The Ministry of Information employed more of them than any other Government department; familiar poets, book-reviewers, writers of detective stories, biographers, publishers, and at least one bibliographer might be met, any night or day of the war, in the great honeycombed tower of London University in Malet Street, preparing news bulletins, censoring books and newspapers, and generally supplying the incessant demand for propaganda. The B.B.C., especially in its overseas and propaganda services, was perhaps the most sympathetic employer from the writer's point of view, for its feature programmes, which included " literary biographies " and broadcast drama, provided him with exceptional opportunities for imaginative writing, of much the same kind as he might have chosen to do on his own initiative in peace-time. Although the literary achievements of the B.B.C. during the war lie outside the scope of this survey, two of them may be mentioned not irrelevantly, as examples of what the conscript writer could produce: Edward Sackville-West's poetic version of the Odyssey, and Louis Macneice's dramatic presentation of the story of Christopher Columbus, both of them since published in book form.

There were many jobs, other than those connected with propaganda and the kind of entertainment discreetly designed to sustain morale and support the general war effort, which requisitioned the brains and pens of the intelligentsia. In those rural communities which throughout the war were veiled in secrecy, and were referred to only by allusive initial capitals, many of the best scholars and men of letters in the country, as well as many of the best teachers from the Universities, were engaged on tasks the nature of which cannot be divulged, but which demanded both special knowledge and the keenest critical perception. It is certain that the output of literary scholarship suffered at the expense of their diverted energies; it is probable that the output of English prose literature in general, and of historical writing in particular, was reduced, both directly and indirectly, for the same reason. One day, perhaps, the common reader will be allowed to read the secret documents of the war and the " histories " of Ministries, which are now being compiled from inexhaustible files and forgotten memoranda by these and other distinguished writers. If so, then it may be that he will yet be given such masterpieces of English prose as will more than compensate for the loss to contemporary English literature of their talents. The prospect, however, is not encouraging. Doubtless many of those who were, and still are, engaged in attempting to reduce vast masses of records to intelligible and readable shape, have no better contribution to make to literature; but, doubtless too, a few of them deserve a better fate than that of expending their creative powers in a waste of official documents.

The pressure of the times and its corollary, the lack of freedom and inclination, were, however, generally unfavourable to the kind of writing which requires preparation or uninterrupted reflection. The steady recollection and integration of experience in tranquillity can rarely be achieved in the enervating vicissitude of war. A few were fortunate enough to work in conditions not altogether inimical to creative writing; a few were entitled by their age or by disablement to the leisure needed for authorship; and some, separated from their families and friends and the distractions of social life, found that writing was a pastime for the unrelieved solitude and monotony of the brief spell between work and sleep. But the majority of those who wrote at all were to find the motive as well as the inclination for writing in the war situation itself. In total war this does not mean writing only about the battle-front. The front-line in modern war stretches back from the tank laagers, the forward airfields, and the warship's action-stations to factories and docks; to slipways and marshalling-yards; to arable and pasture lands; to the patient shopping queue; to the back garden of the humblest " digger for victory ". In all these places, and in the hopes and fears, the active service and passive endurance, of the whole people of Britain at war, they discovered the raw material of literature.

The Solace of Books: travelling library for civil defence workers

Literature for All: 100 million "Penguins" not enough

Stephen Spender: fireman

WRITERS AT WAR

Louis MacNeice: B.B.C. script writer

It would be uncritical to claim that more than a very small number of all the books and pamphlets about the war, published between 1939 and 1945, added anything of permanent value to the treasury of English Letters. Many of these books and pamphlets were officially commissioned for special reasons or occasions; many were written to satisfy public curiosity about an event or subject of particular but ephemeral moment. Throughout the whole period under review propaganda and reportage employed the largest number of pens and typewriters. Something has already been said about the enlistment of writers for preparing propaganda for broadcasting and for mass distribution at home and abroad (including enemy or enemy-occupied territories) in booklet and pamphlet form; the bibliography at the end of this report will give the reader some idea of their work, and of the universal and prodigious labours both of those who were accredited war correspondents and of those who reported their personal experiences on their own initiative.

In the early stages of the war and for some time after German-Japanese aggression had reached its peak, there was a demand for books about the origins and evolution of Fascist ideology in general and of Nazism in particular. The sickly days of appeasement and evasiveness had gone. People wanted to know how and why they had been drawn into the conflict; what were " the evil things " they had been warned, on that first calm September morning of the war, they were fighting against; where they had been conceived and by whom; and what the fearful consequences of their ascendancy might be. In short, who was Hitler and what was Hitlerism. At this stage in the painful process of moral regeneration such curiosity was natural and indeed desirable. There were many writers competent to satisfy it up to the point where knowledge ended and speculation began. The value of the information they provided was necessarily dependent upon first-hand knowledge and experience of Nazi rule, which no one Englishman happily could pretend to possess, as the British Ambassador, Sir Nevile Henderson, for example, so patently proved in his *Failure of a Mission*. They were Europeans who had found refuge in Britain or the U.S.A. and, as such, their work cannot be considered here.

During that period of the war when the tide was turning slowly in favour of the United Nations, curiosity about the past gave way to mixed feelings of apprehension and expectation about the future. This was the moment when, shocked and surfeited by the tale of destruction everywhere, men and women began to dream, if not to think, of rebuilding·from the ruins. The magic words " planning and reconstruction ", which then began to appear on many title-pages, lost much of their fascination when the first dim visions of Utopia had faded, and the reality of a bleak·and almost endless vista of devastation had to be faced. Yet, despite the apathy, disenchantment, and general war-weariness of large numbers of people, the emergence of a responsive social and civic conscience was reflected in the many books and essays on planning and reconstruction written and published in the latter part of the war. There was, indeed, an enormous demand not only for the general thesis and the grand strategic plan for providing social security for all—such as the famous *Beveridge Report*—but also for the " book of instructions " which explained how the broad theoretical principles and articles of faith of, say, the Atlantic Charter could reasonably be expected to work out in practice.

The practice and particularly the theory of agriculture were the subject of many of these treatises on post-war planning—" blueprints ", as they were often inaccurately termed, of a brave new world. It may seem irrelevant to allude to agronomical literature in this record; and so it would be if these treatises had been prompted solely by the need to justify and encourage the intensive cultivation of home-produced foodstuffs after years of deplorable and grossly improvident neglect of the soil. But, in fact, some of them drew their inspiration from far deeper sources, and their conclusions, not from present necessity, but from what their authors believed to be fundamental causes and effects. The most striking of them adumbrated a kind of " mystique " of the soil, based upon a type of pagan reverence for the Mother principle in Nature and deriving from a belief that man's salvation is dependent upon his filial devotion and respect for her. The psychologist might perhaps attribute this obsession with the " living " soil to a subliminal fear and hatred of the destructive potentiality of modern technology

British Museum Library: blitzed book stack

Paternoster Row: six million volumes destroyed in one night (*G. Wren Howard*)

" Except a corn of wheat fall into the ground and die. . . ."

Bomber Command: " Home is where we start from "

which is capable of producing, by similar means and in one and the same factory, tanks and tractors, armoured cars and combine-harvesters, high-explosives and artificial fertilisers. The rise of this religion of the soil in the course of a mechanised war is a phenomenon that deserves closer study. The fervour and sincerity of its evangelists are often impressively transmitted in their writing, endowing it with a literary quality seldom found in scientific text-books.

It is difficult, and at this juncture perhaps unprofitable, to judge whether there was, in the widest sense, any general revival of religious belief during the war. There was undoubtedly a considerable output of devotional as distinct from theological literature, designed more to solace those who seek reassurance from super-natural sources, when earthly comfort fails, than to bring the infidel back to a knowledge of God. At the same time it is worth remarking that in a number of books, not specifically religious, published during the early 1940's, there are signs of a vague spiritual yearning which may or may not be symptomatic of a recrudescence of faith. It remains to be seen whether man's discovery and im-mediate abuse of the cataclysmic energy released by atomic fission will fortify or weaken his transcendental aspirations and noumenal gropings.

Many readers—possibly a majority—seeking an escape from the iron grasp of war-time conditions or, at least, relaxation from their grip, were more easily solaced by autobiographies or biographical studies which either portrayed their subjects against the background of a happier and richer world, or, by setting them among the tribula-tions of their own times, showed that there was as much to be endured in the past as in the present. From this point of view, the reader could console himself with the discovery that life has always been disagreeable, and that he could bear it as bravely as his ancestors. Next to fiction, such books of reminiscence made up the largest part of what was sometimes called " escapist " literature—a term of contempt much fancied by those who contend that literature must be, as the French now say, "engaged", and that the *recherche du temps perdu* is somehow an admission of defeat, a betrayal of the present to the past.

B

Such in broad outline were the principal interests, created more or less directly by the war situation, that provided subjects for English prose writers between 1939 and 1945. In the following pages this outline will be filled in with some particulars and discursive criticism of the most remarkable books published during those years, and not only of those concerned specifically with these topical interests but also of those—far fewer in number—which have no bearing on the war or its current repercussions, but which none the less belong to the continuing tradition of English Letters.

II. THE WAR

The aftermath of a world-wide or " global " war, as those who are old enough to remember the years that followed the armistice of 1918 need not be told, is a period of confused values. In particular, it is extraordinarily difficult to evaluate war literature immediately after the events that inspired and produced it. Thus a great deal of the purely topical, *ad hoc* accounts of war experience, commonly written under pressure and without the benefit of revision or mature deliberation, would seem to have only an ephemeral interest hardly greater, though preserved between the covers of a book, than the diurnal dispatches of war correspondents. Yet it is impossible to feel sure that these eye-witness accounts may not acquire in the future a value which cannot be claimed for them now. Some of them, at least, may survive on their own merits and not merely as source-books for the historian. As in the first world war of 1914–1918, so in the second, the later stages of the struggle were marked by a gradual decline in the popularity of books of this kind; within a few months of the armistice they ceased almost entirely to appeal to the war-weary and war-surfeited reader, and became a drug on the book market. It is probable that this antipathy will continue for some time to come, and that a decade will pass, as it did after November 1918, before there is a revival of interest in war as a subject for prose or poetry. At present, while it is too soon to tell whether anything of permanent literary value will emerge from the mass of " war books " printed between 1939 and

1945, it may be said with some confidence that the events of those years have yet to produce a Blunden or a Sassoon or a Graves.

This is not to say that the war, in all its aspects, at home and abroad, was not extensively, continuously, and sometimes brilliantly reported. It has already been noted that many of the most gifted writers of the day were recruited for this purpose. Some of them, writing under the auspices of the Ministry of Information or the British Council, were assigned the special task of telling Britain's friends overseas something about her history, her institutions, her customs, and her contribution to culture. Others were employed to write up, from official information, authoritative accounts of particular campaigns and events. His Majesty's Stationery Office, as publisher to the Government Departments and especially the Ministry of Information, extended its activities over a wide field of general publishing; and, to the concern and envy of commercial publishers, who had some cause to resent the intrusion of a rival with an unlimited allocation of paper, sponsored a number of " bestsellers ". The authors of these well-printed and lavishly-illustrated volumes were generally anonymous, but the name of one—Hilary St. George Saunders, a civil servant by profession but a novelist by inclination—soon became known. He, more than any other, established the deserved reputation for informed, lucid, and vivid narrative of the official stories of *The Battle of Britain*; *Bomber Command*; *Coastal Command*; and *Roof Over Britain*—the story of the air defences of the British Isles—and others. Similar, if less engrossing, publications covered other outstanding features of the general war effort such as the railroad and transport systems.

From first to last, however, it was the war in the air that captured the imagination of writer and reader alike. It was the one enthralling aspect of operational warfare which the civilian non-combatant could see for himself and in which he could feel himself to be deeply implicated. The fantastic air battles over the approaches to London during the " Battle of Britain " and the siren-heralded air raids were, in the long run, less impressive in this sense than the constant and visible reminder of the country's air potential on the great airfields up and down the land; in the ubiquitous air-crews; and in the moving sight and sound of the squadrons and wings of Bomber

Command climbing through the failing light towards their objectives on the continent of Europe. The early phase, September 1939–May 1941, was reviewed by the well-known novelist and practised aeronaut, David Garnett, in *The War in the Air*. This masterly record, based on official documents and written with impeccable discretion and understanding, is likely to outlast all other commentaries on the same period. It may be noted here that the same writer, who is currently writing a section of the secret history of the war, also wrote the major part of *The War in Greece and Crete*, one of a series, entitled " The Army at War ", issued on behalf of the War Office by the Ministry of Information.

Apart from officially compiled and sponsored records of the three Services and their auxiliaries—including such popular ones as *Front Line* (the story of Civil Defence); *Combined Operations*; *The Eighth Army* (the victors of El Alamein); *Ark Royal* (the Admiralty account of the famous aircraft-carrier's exploits); and *His Majesty's Minesweepers*—there was a considerable output of books written by individual serving men (a few also by women) about their personal experiences. The best of these were the professional work of war correspondents, like Alan Moorehead, whose two books—*African Trilogy* and *Eclipse*, covering the African, Italian, and Western campaigns, are not only strikingly descriptive of incident but also succeed, as few other writers on the spot succeeded, in conveying what fighting meant to the average soldier. Certainly in no other book of similar scope are the *servitudes et grandeurs militaires* of a modern army so profoundly discerned or so graphically portrayed.

Too many of these personal records, it must be frankly admitted, are little more than collections of inconsequent anecdotes, dashed down on paper by men who had almost every kind of qualification except the essential one of knowing how to write about them. This failure is most evident in the reminiscences of airmen who, because their adventures were without precedent and their lives a strange blend of relatively comfortable security on earth and fearful jeopardy in the sky, were more prolific writers than soldiers or sailors. It is not entirely redeemed in the best known of all the books directly inspired by personal experience of air warfare—*The*

Alan Moorehead: war correspondent

Richard Hillary: fighter pilot in the Battle of Britain

Rt. Hon. John Strachey, P.C.: Air Raid Warden, 1940, Under Secretary of State, 1945

H. St. George Saunders: Official Chronicler

Last Enemy, by Richard Hillary, one of the few fighter-pilots to whom
so many owed so much in the Battle of Britain. This moving
testament of youth, grown old beyond its years in single-handed
combat with the enemy, is the kind of book which disarms criticism.
The obvious defects of its qualities are too firmly woven into the
emotional pattern to be isolated without damaging the texture
of the work as a whole. There is, furthermore, the difficulty of
estimating how much its appeal owes to the existence, in embryo,
of a "Hillary" myth. Like Rupert Brooke in the first world
war, Richard Hillary in the second has been chosen as a sym-
bol of youth's tragic destiny and unfulfilled promise. To say that
The Last Enemy plays on these themes with a freshness and poignancy
which abler writers may indeed envy, is not to say that it does so
with complete success. The superiority of method and accomplish-
ment of a practised writer, faced with the issues of life and death,
is obvious, for instance, in the work of Arthur Koestler, an Austrian
journalist and author, incidentally, of the essay "Birth of a Myth"
which initiated the apotheosis of Hillary. Koestler's *Scum of the
Earth* and *Darkness at Noon*—passionate, disabused, yet authentic
studies of the outcast, the dispossessed, and the refugee—deserve
to be mentioned here, though, strictly, they lie outside the scope
of this record.

The skill an experienced writer can exercise in the purely objec-
tive statement of extraordinary occurrences was strikingly used by
John Strachey in his still uncollected articles on the R.A.F., and out-
standingly so in *Post D*, a bare narration of rescue work during the
London Blitz—in its classic simplicity and sobriety one of the few
memorable records by an eye-witness of one of the minor disasters
of war. Something of the same temper and refinement is found
in the story of the evacuation of the overwhelmed but undefeated
British Army from Dunkirk, entitled *The Nine Days' Wonder*, by the
Poet Laureate, John Masefield. It is worth adding, as a final
example of professional skill—in this case that of a journalist para-
chuted into France to help the French underground Resistance
Movement—George Millar's *Maquis*. Millar was attached to the
Resistance Movement, not as a reporter but as a soldier and saboteur,
and his tale, written after his safe return, has no pretensions to be

anything but an exciting, picaresque piece of autobiography. As such, however, it has a sound claim to be considered the best personal adventure story of the war.

On the whole it is probably true that more literary energy was put indirectly into the general war effort than directly into the writing of books about the war. It is significant that the most eminent of living English writers, apart from the few who were officially delegated to write about specific aspects of the war, did not allow themselves to be diverted from their proper studies. Their names will appear in the following sections associated with the subjects they have always professed. But, before concluding this section, it is fitting to crown its end with a reference to the five volumes of Winston Churchill's war-time orations in and out of Parliament: *Into Battle*; *The Unrelenting Struggle*; *The End of the Beginning*; *Onwards to Victory*; and *The Dawn of Liberation*—the very titles of which echo his predilection for the sonorous elements in a language of whose emotional resources he is the most accomplished exponent living.

III. BIOGRAPHY AND AUTOBIOGRAPHY

Like Nature in Tennyson's view, so total war seems " careless of the single life ". In the struggle for survival the individual, regimented, directed, and controlled at work and play, is forced to submerge his identity, and sacrifice, in the common interest, much of his freedom of action. There is some irony in the fact that as soon as war broke out every man, woman, and child in the British Isles was issued, for the first time, with an Identity Card—as if, without one, individuality might cease to exist. It is arguable that a consequence of this change in the human condition was the widespread interest shown during the war in books about people as individuals. The publication of an unusually large number of auto-biographies certainly suggests that, for want of other outlets, there was a more than ordinary readiness among writers to assert their personalities in print. It has already been suggested that there was also a desire, among readers, to escape out of the present into the past; to recall the old days that always seem good in retrospect; to identify themselves with a personality. And, it may be remarked, there was exceptional opportunity for writing and reading autobiography for those whose age or infirmity prevented them from taking an active part in the war and who, more than younger men and women, have a right to indulge in reminiscence.

Amongst these, as one would expect, were the senior members of the Universities of Oxford and Cambridge, where life, even in war-time, pursues, or, with some slight adjustment, can be made to seem to pursue, its calm accustomed way. Characteristic of the autobiographies of this secluded class are *Memories of Victorian Oxford*, by the eminent historian Sir Charles Oman, and *55 Years at Oxford*, by G. B. Grundy, a typical " don " of the older generation. Such books, offspring of mellow and placid minds, preserve in an endearing fashion an illusion of permanence and stability in a changing and convulsed society. Something of the same quality, but quickened by urbanity and polished by contact with the outside world, is found in the posthumously-edited *Letters* of George Gordon, former President of Magdalen College, a scholar and essayist, who wrote far less than he would have done, had Oxford not lulled him by her enchantments into a state of hebetude, as she has so many of her resident lovers. Even in *Short Journey*, the autobiography of Professor E. L. Woodward, a younger man who fought in the Four Years' War and travelled extensively before settling down at Oxford, this element of unreality flavoured with parochialism is pervasive. It is odd that Cambridge, more provincial, at least superficially, than Oxford, is less prone to this kind of self-indulgence, though it is fair to add that nothing written at Oxford can be compared for insipidity and narrowness with *Letters from Cambridge*, a series of monthly bulletins circulated by A. S. F. Gow, a Fellow of Trinity College, to his friends and former pupils.

It is as well that writers are not required to indicate in the titles of their memoirs the relative insignificance of their lives; for, if they were, it would be difficult to place, in relation to those of the University gossips, Bishop Hensley Henson's *Retrospect of an Unimportant Life*. Considered *sub specie aeternitatis*, Dr. Henson's distinguished and influential career in the Church may turn out to have been "unimportant", but it is a misleading qualification on the title-page of a book written, presumably, to interest those who have no authority to pass judgement.   Here it is only necessary to praise the skill with which he describes the progress of his disabused spirit through the shoals and narrows and storms of an arduous and often frustrated voyage through life.   Dr. Henson, who has been called the greatest preacher of his generation, is also one of the few living masters of English prose.   By the beauty, vitality, and character of its style alone, his autobiography must be considered one of the out-standing books produced during the war.   Intellectually and spiritually, *The Confession of an Octogenarian*, by Dr. L. P. Jacks, for many years a revered editor of the philosophic *Hibbert Journal*, has a certain affinity with Dr. Henson's autobiography; but they are the recollections and confidences of an old man, and give the impression of having been compiled with effort too late in life.

The fact that a number of well-known men of letters wrote their autobiographies during the war years suggests that, apart from the natural urge to retrospect and reminiscence exerted by force of circumstance, it was easier for them to write about themselves than about anything else, the crystallised past being so much more transpicuous than the turbulent present.   There were, of course, entertaining autobiographies written by men and women eminent in many walks of life, but not authors by profession, such as *A Mingled Chime*, by the aggressive conductor Sir Thomas Beecham, or the three volumes—*Commando*, *Trekking On*, and *No Out-Span*—by that vigorous man of action, the late Denys Reitz, High Commis-sioner for South Africa.   But for the purpose of this survey, it is the autobiographies of professed writers which are of particular interest and significance.

In a sense, a creative writer who turns to autobiography too soon is living on the capital of his experiences and runs the risk of using up raw material which could be more profitably incorporated in poetry, fiction, or some other literary *genre*.   It may be that, during the first half of the war when the future for any kind of literature seemed desperately uncertain, there seemed to some writers little point in attempting to preserve this accumulated capital.   It had been saved in happier conditions, which they then supposed would never return, and it was apparently bound to depreciate further and further in value. Even after the end of the war it was obvious that the break with the pre-war period was irreparable, and that a reorientation of intelligence and sensibility, a recapitalisation of experience, was inevitable.

This, it may be contended, was in fact a stronger motive for self-portraiture than the mere soothing pastime of evoking scenes and experiences of infancy and youth. The charm of such early reminiscence—the rapture of the backward view—is nevertheless beautifully expressed in Herbert Read's *Annals of Innocence*; in Sean O'Casey's Joycean trilogy of his drab yet picaresque Dublin childhood and young rebel-hood; in Lord Berners's account of patrician schooldays at Eton; in William Plomer's *Double Lives* in South Africa, England, and the Far East; in F. D. Ommanney's *The House in the Park*; and most attractively in the first of four volumes—*Left Hand, Right Hand!*—of Sir Osbert Sitwell's spacious and serene memoirs of a vanished epoch and a submerged aristocracy. Yet none of these admirable studies is motivated by the sense of urgency, by the desire to set down before it is too late, unrecapturable emotion, that characterises a singularly revealing fragment of self-analysis, published during the autumn of 1944, with the title *The Unquiet Grave* and over the pseudonym " Palinurus ". There are many people, including some judicious critics, who consider that this curious " word-cycle ", so original in substance and form as to be hardly classifiable, is the most important piece of English prose literature produced during the war. There are others who have dismissed it as the self-advertisement of a decadent, morbidly introspective " neurotic "; and among them, significantly, is Charles Morgan, who, throughout the war, styling himself " Menander " and acting the part of arbiter of literary values and good taste, laid down the literary law each week in the pages of *The Times Literary Supplement*. No work of the period, at all events, has provoked livelier or more intelligent discussion among the critically-minded. Its merits and faults have been widely debated—to the dismay, doubtless, of its detractors, who, having dismissed the book in its original limited issue as the darling of a coterie, were to see 20,000 copies of two ordinary editions sold out on publication. By that time

" Palinurus " had been identified as Cyril Connolly, editor of the literary monthly *Horizon*, and leader of the intellectual *avant-garde*.

Whatever disapproval (or resentment) may be felt about the symbolic Palinurus's tendency to self-commiseration and regretful yearning for his lost life and happiness, it is impossible to deny the skill with which he blends love of literature (expressed in exquisitely organised quotation) with love of life (evoked in description of places and experience). With the exception of the autobiographical element in Evelyn Waugh's novel *Brideshead Revisited*, no memoir of recent years conveys more faithfully or more potently the personal dilemma of the intellectuals who grew up between the two wars, and the romantic agony of their disillusioned and disoriented spirits. But *The Unquiet Grave* possesses other qualities which may ultimately prove to be its best preservative against oblivion. It is written in prose that is always perfectly fitted to the subject it is required to express; the changing moods of the author are reflected without distortion in the polished style. Few contemporary writers care so much about language as Connolly; know so much about its resources; use them with such respect. It is also that anomaly—rare enough still, notwithstanding the ease and speed of modern travel, but even more so during the war when Britain was completely isolated from the Continent—a work of art by an English writer with a cosmopolitan outlook. In the published work of no other British contemporary can one detect more strongly than in Connolly's the influence of European and, especially, Mediterranean culture. Compared with *The Unquiet Grave*, the most discursive and delightful of modern autobiographies seem, if not positively provincial, at least insular and all too self-contained.

During the uneasy armistice between the wars, literary and historical biography was already a flourishing industry. What particular economic and psychological forces were concerned in its mass-production cannot be investigated here: it is enough to say that the demand created a steady supply; that few writers did not try their hand at biography; that even the best were urged by their publishers to work for this profitable market. The supply inevitably declined during the war; there was a shortage of biographers as well as of everything else. In general, it can be said that there were no outstanding achievements in this field. The ironic method of Lytton Strachey, employed by Philip Guedalla (who died in 1944) and, misguidedly, by many busy denigrators, had fallen into disrepute before the war; in its place biographers developed the straightforward method of conventional portraiture by adding " psychological interpretation "—a dubious benefit—which was as often as not hypothetical and impertinent; or, imitating the French technique, constructed, with the aid of speculations, fictions and imaginary conversations, *vies romantiques*, which are commonly a great deal more " romantic " than lifelike. The best in this kind is undoubtedly Peter Quennell, whose *Byron in Italy*, and *Four Portraits* of Boswell, Gibbon, Sterne, Wilkes, may be singled out because they are the work of a portraitist with a penetrating eye for character and personality and a lively sense of social and aesthetic values. It is perhaps a matter of regret that these gifts, to which must be added an exceptional sensibility to language,—so finely used in his early study of *Baudelaire and the Symbolists*,—should latterly have been squandered too freely on literary journalism. The bastard *genre* of the romanticised novel-biography, of which Margaret Irwin is probably the most talented living exponent, though there are several other women who are hardly less proficient, cannot be discussed here.

The most commendable examples of well-documented biography published between 1939 and 1945 were Virginia Woolf's *Life* of Roger Fry, a study by one artist of exquisite sensibility of another; Joseph Hone's *Life* of W. B. Yeats, which was authorised by the poet's family and is consequently somewhat restrained; Hesketh Pearson's intimate *Life* of Bernard Shaw, a valuable but unco-ordinated collection of facts, in this respect similar to Herbert Gorman's biography of James Joyce or Grant Richards's personal memoir of A. E. Housman; and Lord Ponsonby's fascinating *Life and Letters* of his father Sir Henry Ponsonby, Queen Victoria's private secretary.

Only one historical biography of the period, which produced imposing new biographies of, for example, Hazlitt, Southey, and Dickens, deserves particular mention. This is Aldous Huxley's *Grey Eminence*, a subtle analysis of the character and career of the obscure but sinister figure of the Father Joseph who subserved Cardinal Richelieu's designs. It demonstrates with exemplary skill the capital truth, which every generation in a Christian society is bound to acknowledge, that it is not possible to serve both God and Mammon faithfully. In the individual case of Father Joseph it illustrates the disastrous consequences of divided loyalty in a man who, in an attempt to integrate religious faith and duty with a system of ruthless power politics, lost his soul yet gained no earthly reward for his pains. The moral of this profound study of spiritual decadence was probably missed or at least overlooked by many of its readers at the date of its publication. Certainly the sermon preached by Huxley on his Californian mount was not easy to attend to on the occasion of its delivery, and was even a little re-sented by those who in the zone of war were less comfortably and securely placed than he for the calm and detached contemplation of the eternal verities. Its significance, for our own time, is un-likely to be fully realised until spiritual values, miscalculated, neglected or discarded in the confusion of war, are reaffirmed, and the life of the spirit once again resumed. Whether this remarkable book has made or is likely to make any converts to Huxley's private religion of neo-Brahminism, the tenets of which are ingeniously interwoven with the fabric of his story, is another question, and one that cannot be answered here.

IV. ESSAYS AND CRITICISM

For various reasons, which deserve a moment's attention, literary criticism and the literary essay were more widely cultivated during the war years than any other form of serious prose literature. In the first place, there were more frequent opportunities for this kind of occasional writing than there were for more extended and laborious work. It would be hardly worth remarking that a critical essay requires a relatively small amount of time or prolonged thought spent on its composition, if it were not desirable to emphasise how little of either most writers could afford to spare under war con-ditions. In passing it may be said that, low as the standard of book-

Winston Churchill, O.M., in the Cabinet Room, No. 10 Downing Street

Sir Osbert Sitwell, Bart.

Cyril Connolly: a leader of the literary *avant-garde*

reviewing was throughout the war even in the most reputable journals, it would have been lower still if the average had not been raised by a few experienced critics who could still undertake to write a few hundred words—the paper shortage imposed this limit —after their long day's war work was done. Secondly, there were, by and large, more writers available and qualified to do this kind of work.

Although the Universities and other learned institutions, which are normally the principal centres of critical activity, were deprived of many of their liveliest minds,—an authority on Chaucer, for example, being seconded to the Ministry of Food; a professor of English literature, turned colonel, being transferred to the Bureau of Army Education; a philosopher enlisting as an ensign in the Welsh Guards; and so on,—a proportion remained behind, and had at least as much opportunity as in peace-time for casual literary pursuits. Further, it was the policy of the Ministry of Labour and National Service to classify literary editorship as a " reserved occupa- tion", and so permit a responsible man of letters to remain, as it were, on literary duty with any newspaper or periodical accustomed to employ one.

Although life at Oxford and Cambridge, during the war, was complicated and disturbed by the heavy demands for accommoda- tion and educational facilities made by evacuated Government departments and evacuated faculties of London·University; by the Services for the training of air-crews and for short-term politico- military courses on Military Government; and by the special needs of scientific research—both Universities, and Oxford in particular, made noteworthy contributions to literary criticism. Even when allowance is made for the fact that much of what was published must have been planned, and perhaps partly written, before the war, it is still gratifying to be able to record the appearance, within the space of five years, of such books as Dr. C. M. Bowra's *The Heritage of Symbolism* and *From Virgil to Milton*; Dr. E. M. W. Tillyard's *The Elizabethan World Picture* and *Shakespeare's History Plays*; Lord David Cecil's *Hardy the Novelist* ; Basil Willey's *The Eighteenth Century Background*; and C. S. Lewis's *Preface to " Paradise Lost "*.

The range and acuity of Dr. Bowra's critical eye are especially

remarkable. These attributes, it is true, are not altogether exceptional, for C. S. Lewis is not less gifted in this respect; but whereas
Lewis has tended progressively to survey literature from a point of
view fixed for him by his religious principles, which predispose him
to treat it and its relation to life as a department of morals rather
than as material for intellectual and aesthetic criticism, Bowra
moves freely over the whole field of literary achievement without
prejudice or preconceived notions of its ultimate purpose or significance. Like David Cecil, Bowra is above all concerned with the
writer as artist, and with his books as works of art. His criticism
is essentially humanistic, deeply rooted in and nourished by the
civilisation of ancient Greece. It is as unusual as it is welcome to
find a professed classical scholar competent to write with authority
as well as enthusiasm on subjects as various as the European epic and
contemporary European poetry. Bowra's studies of the post-
Symbolists, Paul Valéry, Rainer Maria Rilke, Stefan Georg, and
Alexander Blok, are the best introduction in English to their works
and, perhaps, the most illuminating general survey, in any language,
of the later phases of the Symbolist Movement. Such wide-ranging
exploration of Continental literature is especially profitable for the
English reader, who is too readily inclined to insulate himself from
European influences. Moreover, the English-speaking peoples
should be grateful to any critic capable of arousing a sympathetic
interest in the poetry of the Soviet Union. It need hardly be said
here that, if civilisation is to survive in the " atomic age ", it is
imperative that there should be the fullest possible cultural understanding between nations, and not least between the English-
speaking world and the still remote Union of Soviet Socialist
Republics.

Dr. Bowra's inclusion of Milton, with Virgil, Tasso, and Camöens,
in his enlightened defence of the Epic, was one sign among several
of revived interest in Miltonic criticism. It may be that such
criticism directly encouraged some people to read or re-read
Paradise Lost, and this would account in part for the popularity of
Milton's poetry during the war; but it would be more reasonable
to attribute this vogue to the desire to resolve prevailing moods of
doubt, despair, and spiritual longing, than to the stimulus of the

critics. The significant fact remains that some of the best critical interpretation and revaluation of the period under review was inspired by Milton's poetry and prose. The most illuminating of these critical essays are concerned more with Milton's ideology and poetic sensibility than with textual appreciation and exegesis. Professor Saurat's *Milton, Man and Thinker*, for example, is a deeply-informed investigation of Milton's theological and philosophical background; Charles Williams's remarkable introductory essay to the *Minor Poems* (in " The World's Classics ") deduces from *Comus* a concept of chastity, which this greatly lamented critic developed further in an esoteric analysis of the sexual relationship in his *Figure of Beatrice* (Dante's Beatrice); while C. S. Lewis's *Preface to Paradise Lost*, which contains, incidentally, one of the finest appreciations of Virgil in the English language, analyses the " epic " nature of the poem and its spiritual and theological content. Wilson Knight's characteristically romantic study, *Chariot of Wrath*, must also be mentioned, along with the late Logan Pearsall Smith's lapidary, provocative, if slightly peevish, *Milton and his Modern Critics*. This stalwart defence of the poet by a great patrician and trustee of English letters was directed primarily against an earlier attack on Milton made by Dr. F. R. Leavis, the cold, intellectual leader of a minority group of Cambridge critics whose methodical and uncompromising destruction of reputations periodically enlivens the pages of their hypercritical but bracing magazine *Scrutiny*.

In other and more fruitful ways the University of Cambridge was responsible during the war for some important works of literary criticism. Some of these—notably *The Elizabethan World Picture* and *Shakespeare's History Plays*, by Dr. E. M. W. Tillyard, himself the author of a valuable critical study of Milton; Joan Bennett's small but sensitive monograph on *Virginia Woolf*; and Basil Willey's masterly *The Eighteenth Century Background*—were by resident members of the English Faculty. The best of them, such as the examples mentioned, are singularly free from the limitations and pedantry which commonly disfigure academic dissertations. Others were, so to speak, commissioned by the University from esteemed critics outside its ancient walls. Pre-eminent amongst these were the collections, some as yet unpublished, of the annual " Clark Lectures ",

which were maintained throughout the war and included an in-
genious interpretation of the character of Falstaff, by Professor
Dover Wilson, the Shakespearian scholar; Lord David Cecil's deli-
cately sympathetic appraisal of the art and philosophy of Thomas
Hardy, the last of Britain's regional novelists; C. S. Lewis's wide-
ranging and allusive commentary on English life and letters in the
sixteenth century; and Raymond Mortimer's witty and sophisticated
reflections on a group of Victorian " dissidents "—Bagehot, Fitz-
Gerald, Pater, and Meredith.

Elsewhere than at Oxford and Cambridge some critical activity
was maintained, though it appears to have consisted chiefly in com-
pleting books begun well before the outbreak of war, or in collect-
ing scattered essays and addresses for publication in volume form.
To the former class belong two critical investigations of considerable
value—Professor David Douglas's *English Scholars*, an exception-
ally well-written account of the men (and one woman) who, in
the early part of the eighteenth century, undertook a systematic
research into the origins and antiquities of England and the
English; and Humphry House's *The Dickens World*, a sociological
enquiry of absorbing interest in which the author relates the fictitious world of Dickens's novels to the actual conditions of society
in Dickens's lifetime. House's comparative study effectively
exemplifies a trend in recent literary criticism which seems likely
to become more pronounced in the future. Its purpose, very briefly,
is to correlate life and letters, and thus to ascertain and
establish, more firmly than is commonly realised, their inter-rela-
tionship and inter-dependence. This critical method will doubtless
be deplored by those who regard the art of literature as a subject
only for intellectual and aesthetic apprehension; but it is one which
will surely attract more students and exponents as the social revolution of our time proceeds. It is a method, incidentally, which may
well be promoted by the findings of such detective agencies as
" Mass-Observation ", whose intriguing " documentaries " of the
British people at work and play contain the crude substance of
innumerable novels, biographies, and essays. Although it may
not add greatly to the delight of literature, it can add substantially
to its general validity as description of the human condition. It

Dr. C. M. Bowra: Professor of Poetry, Warden of
Wadham College, Oxford

Lord David Cecil: biographer and critic

George Orwell: critic of literature and society

D. W. Brogan: expert on International Relations

might do this, for instance, by revealing the economic conditions prevalent in, say, Shakespeare's England, or, more precisely, by calculating the amount of small beer consumed by the agricultural labourer in Berkshire, when *The Merry Wives of Windsor* was produced by the Lord Chamberlain's servants " before her Majestie and Else-where " at the turn of the sixteenth century. Something of the possibilities of this method was shown in a book by L. C. Knights, published in 1937 under the title *Drama and Society in the Age of Jonson*.

Among the several volumes of papers and addresses published by professed scholars and teachers between 1939 and 1945 may be mentioned Geoffrey Tillotson's scholarly *Essays in Criticism and Research*; the late T. R. Glover's humanistic *Springs of Hellas and other Essays*; Sir Herbert Grierson's *Collected Essays and Addresses*, a volume worthier of this admired critic than the laboured *Critical History of English Poetry* he compiled with J. C. Smith; A. L. Rowse's patriotic *The English Spirit*; and Francis Scarfe's undiscriminating yet helpful guide to contemporary poetry, *Auden and After*. Such collections, to say no more, at least prove the existence and continuity, in unpropitious conditions, of academic criticism.

Generally speaking, however, the academic critic is much less affected than the man of letters or the literary journalist by the modulations of contemporary thought and sensibility. This distinction was more than usually marked during the war, when periodical essay-writing and literary journalism could only be practised under difficulties, which were heavier and more distracting than any the learned had to contend with in their cloistered retreats. Nevertheless a few memorable volumes of essays were put together by such leading reviewers as V. S. Pritchett (*In My Good Books*), who contributed regularly throughout the war to the *New Statesman and Nation*; Raymond Mortimer (*Channel Packet*), literary editor of the same intellectual weekly and the senior liaison officer between French and British literary circles; Cyril Connolly (*The Condemned Playground*), founder and editor of the monthly review *Horizon* in which much of the best occasional writing of the war was printed; and Charles Morgan (*Reflections in a Mirror*), the literary pontiff and spiritual director of studies of the conventional " reading public ".

Some of the best periodical writing of the period was produced by G. M. Young, an elder critic and historian of encyclopaedic knowledge and rare percipience; and by George Orwell (*Critical Essays*), intellectually the most mature critic of the generation that grew up between the two wars. G. M. Young's articles and reviews have yet to be collected and published in book form.

Some miscellaneous volumes of criticism must be added to complete this list: Louis MacNeice's *The Poetry of W. B. Yeats*, a younger poet's examination of the work of the greatest poetic genius of the century; Herbert Read's *Coat of Many Colours*, which covers with exemplary understanding and taste a wide range of problems concerned with current reactions to literature, art, politics, architecture, and society; and Virginia Woolf's posthumous *The Death of the Moth and other Essays*, a selection of critical fragments of unequal merit, but all alike instinct with her characteristic, elusive charm.

At present it is not possible to make a final estimate of T. S. Eliot's service to literary criticism during the war. Although he increased his unchallenged reputation as a poet by the publication in 1943 of *Four Quartets*, the scattered essays and addresses composed by him on various occasions since 1939—notably his lectures on Johnson's *Lives of the Poets*—have not yet been collected, and, until they are, there would be little point in trying to assess, piecemeal, how much they have enhanced his no less outstanding reputation as a critic. A few were published separately, among them *The Classics and the Man of Letters*, the presidential address for 1942 to the Classical Association, and *What is a Classic?*, the first presidential address to the Virgil Society. Both these official discourses revealed an intensified preoccupation with the tradition of European culture, which had been a principal article of Eliot's critical faith many years before he publicly affirmed, in 1928, that he was a " classicist " in literature. The importance that Eliot attaches to the integral relationship of English literature and Continental culture was perhaps intentionally emphasised by his permitting an essay he wrote in 1944 for *The Norseman*, entitled " The Man of Letters and the Future of Europe ", to be reprinted in three other periodicals in Britain, France, and the U.S.A. respectively. The subject had been raised in an earlier address to the Anglo-

Swedish Society in 1943 on " The Nature of Cultural Relations ",
and is due to be treated more comprehensively in a work, still in
progress, some fragments of which have been printed in the form
of " Notes Towards a Definition of Culture ", in *The New English
Weekly*. The essay, " Cultural Forms in the Human Order ", published in the symposium *Prospects for Christendom* (1943), is presumably part of the same thesis.

The special attention paid here to Eliot's fragmentary criticism
would hardly be justified if it were not for the exceptional authority
he wields, both as a critic and as a poet, over the whole field of
contemporary literature. His influence is paramount on his own
generation, on its immediate successor—the generation of such
writers as Auden, Spender, MacNeice, Day Lewis, and Empson—and
on the young. No English writer living is more revered by his
admirers or, it may be added, more respected by his critics. None,
in his writing, has done more to create the climate of thought and
sensibility which has conditioned the form and content of English
literature in the past quarter of a century.

V. HISTORY AND POLITICS

In recent years, the writing of history, at least by professional
historians, has tended to become more and more specialised and to
consist of highly technical analyses of material, suitable for publication only in learned journals. It is conceivable that this method
of scientific investigation and exposition of historical facts and ideas
—by the specialist for the specialist—will in future turn written
history into a series of articles and monographs which none but the
experts will bother to read. If this melancholy prognostic should
prove to be correct, the art of the historian (if art it can be called)
will be superseded by the laborious inductions of the statistician,
the economist, or the research worker who knows every fluctuation
in the price of potatoes between one year's end and the next. It
would mean the end of writing such expansive books as Professor
G. M. Trevelyan's *English Social History* which has delighted scores
of thousands of readers since its publication in 1944, by its broad

and animated delineation of five centuries of domestic life; or Arthur Bryant's *English Saga*, which recounts, less completely and reliably, the story of the English people during the hundred years between 1840 and 1940.

While the professional historians are accumulating material, which by its diffuseness will become progressively harder to assimilate, and wrestling with their occupational doubts—the validity of "The Whig Interpretation of History" and so forth—it is to be hoped that, in the interest of the common reader, inconsiderable though this may seem to them to be, history may yet continue to be written for entertainment as well as instruction.

Much of the history written and published between 1939 and 1945 was concerned to distinguish and define the general as well as the particular factors—political, economic, social—that had determined or rather had seemed to determine, the course of events leading up to the outbreak of war. Some studies, like Harold Butler's *The Lost Peace* and Arthur Bryant's *Unfinished Victory*, sought to discover the causes of the second world war in the failure of the victors of the first to create the requisite conditions of peace. *The Conditions of Peace* was the title, incidentally, of an important book by E. H. Carr, designed to inform public opinion in time to prevent, if this were humanly possible, the same disastrous mistakes being made by the peacemakers twice in a generation. Others, like *The Long Week-end*—an ironical title which only the "week-ending" Englishman will appreciate—by Robert Graves, a poet and historian of the Four Years' War, in collaboration with Alan Hodge; and *Time Exposure*, a photographic survey by Cecil Beaton, with a running commentary by Peter Quennell, were intended to refresh people's memories of how they whiled away their time in society between the spring of 1919 and the autumn of 1939—the record, for better or for worse, of twenty years' aimless drifting between two catastrophes.

Those two decades of undeclared war witnessed the collapse of the League of Nations, the growth of isolationism in the western hemisphere, the increasing trend towards autarky, and the rise of aggressive nationalism. In this hopeless state of international anarchy, the principles of collective security and "federal union"

T. S. Eliot: Stockholm 1942, lecturing for the British Council

Raymond Mortimer: critic

LITERARY JOURNALISM

V. S. Pritchett: novelist and critic

which were passionately held but vainly advocated by many idealists with left-wing attachments and sympathies during the 1930's, when a re-declaration of war was only a matter of time, had no chance of being adopted.   Even after the fighting had been resumed, the urgent need for international co-operation seemed for a while no nearer fulfilment.   Europe, overrun by the Nazis, was isolated; France had fallen; the U.S.A. was still hesitating to commit herself; the Soviet Union had temporised.   After the retreat from Dunkirk, Britain and the Commonwealth were alone.   The events of the year 1940 added an illustrious but sombre passage to English history, comparable in kind, though immeasurably greater in degree, with the emergency created by Napoleon's threat of invasion.   The analogy was ably drawn by a number of writers; by Carola Oman, for example, in *Britain against Napoleon*, and by Arthur Bryant in *The Years of Endurance, 1793–1802*, and its sequel *The Years of Victory, 1802–1814*.   It was not until the Soviet Union and the U.S.A. entered the war that the solidarity of the United Nations became a matter of expediency, and that an identification of self-interest revived at least temporarily the spirit of internationalism.

This revival was marked in Britain by a desire to know and to be known.   The British wanted to learn about foreign countries and their peoples, and at the same time "to tell the world" something about themselves.   A great deal of what was written for the enlightenment of the foreigner was deliberate propaganda, sponsored by the Ministry of Information, and it is perhaps surprising that it was so effective, seeing that the British, though not averse from self-esteem, dislike drumming their virtues into those who cannot clearly see them for themselves.   The series "Britain in Pictures", comprising a hundred volumes and more, and covering, briefly yet authoritatively, almost every aspect of British life and thought, is (although primarily a commercial venture) an outstanding example of such discreet self-advertisement, which it is the business of the British Council to foster and to spread abroad.   On the other hand the desire for information about the world at large, stimulated by the long geography lesson of universal war, and excited more immediately for many people in Great Britain by the presence in their towns, villages, and homes of foreign governments, soldiers, and civilian refugees, was partially satisfied by several excellent series of essays, of which the largest and most widely distributed is the one entitled *Oxford Pamphlets on World Affairs*. Written by experts, they combine together to form a kind of concise encyclopaedia of foreign affairs, from which the bare essentials of geography, geo-politics, economics, and so forth may be learned without tears.

Professor D. W. Brogan, whose *Development of Modern France*, published early in the war, is acknowledged to be the most comprehensive political history of the Third Republic, boldly undertook and successfully achieved the task of explaining the Americans to the British and the British to the Americans. In this dual role he could speak frankly to both peoples without causing offence, because, though he lives in England and has stayed long in the U.S.A., he claims that only Scottish and Irish blood flows in his veins. *The American Problem* and *The English People* are both penetrating analyses of national character and national characteristics; Britons and Americans, indeed, are as likely to learn from them as much about themselves as about each other. Professor Brogan shows, in both these books, that he is better aware than most publicists of the importance, for international understanding, of the people of one country seeing themselves as the people of other countries see them.

In a phase of man's history when mutual respect and tolerance, the cardinal elements of peace, are hard to seek, such aids are likely to prove more cogent and effectual in the short yet critical run of the post-war years, while the abuse of atomic energy threatens him with annihilation, than such learned theorisings on politics as Sir Ernest Barker's *Essays on Government* or G. P. Gooch's *Studies in Diplomacy*. They will surely prove more fruitful, in the long run too, than the trenchant animadversions against the common enemy which Lord Vansittart, a man of peace notwithstanding, poured forth in book and pamphlet throughout the war.

Whenever and wherever there are infamous things in the world to be uprooted and destroyed, satire, almost a lost art in English hands—but in any hands perhaps too slender a weapon now to defeat the manifold enemies of society—can accomplish as much, if not more, and with less risk of repercussion, than the primitive clamour for revenge. In this belief, presumably, George Orwell wrote his fable, *Animal Farm*, the keenest flash of satire that pierced the prevailing gloom of the six years of war. Swift's " race of little odious vermin " were not more pernicious than Orwell's latter-day swine, who ordained that " All animals are born equal: but some animals are born more equal than others ".

VI. RELIGION, PHILOSOPHY, SCIENCE, SCHOLARSHIP

In a world controlled, to all immediate intents and purposes, by the power for good and evil that applied science has placed in men's hands, spiritual values have progressively declined. It is a commonplace of the pulpit and platform that scientific invention, in a few decades, has surpassed the halting moral progress mankind has made in twenty centuries. More and more importance is now attached to means; less and less significance to ends. The first use in 1945 of atomic energy—to wipe out an entire community of men, women, and children—was an ominous and alarming symptom of this dangerous, perhaps fatal, disease of the human spirit. Widespread contempt of the moral law has led, in Great Britain at least, to a corresponding decay of religious belief and religious practice. The Church of England, though " by law established "—a phrase which must have bewildered many foreigners—has no authority, spiritual or temporal, such as the Church of Rome has, to compel its members to worship; in recent years, consequently, its influence has greatly deteriorated. To judge only by its absence from church, the younger generation would appear to be almost wholly without religion. Such evidence is not, of course, conclusive; and it would be ingenuous to assume, even on the corroborative evidence of youth's worldliness, that it altogether lacks faith of some sort in its spiritual destiny. That a desire for it exists in some souls is evident from the recent increase in the numbers of those who have found anchorage in the Roman Church, and of those who, seeking spiritual discipline, have obtained it in the Anglo-Catholic movement.

The precarious state of religious belief and religious observance in Britain was examined with profound concern by writers, both of the clergy and laity, during the war years when, inevitably, moral standards were still further depreciated. Their diagnoses and prognoses tend to vary according to the emphasis they place, individually and collectively, on the sociological or theological aspects of the case. The latter were debated during 1944 in a plenary session of clergy and laity at Malvern—later the research centre for radiolocation—and its divergent conclusions published in *Malvern 1941* and its sequel *Malvern and After*. The former were lucidly and incisively demonstrated by the late Archbishop of Canterbury, William Temple, in a tract, entitled *Christianity and the Social Order*, which was published and widely distributed by " Penguin Books ". Temple, whose untimely death was an irreparable loss to the Church and indeed to society at large, was reproached, in certain quarters, with meddling in politics and economics when he condemned the profit motive of the money-changers and called for better housing and health. His conception of a Christian society, in which charity, amongst other things, was to begin at home and in the home, encouraged a hope that the Church of England was about to put its own house, and the people's houses, in order. That hope might have been realised more quickly had he lived to collaborate with Britain's first secure socialist government. To the layman it must seem strange that he had critics in the Church itself, in that section, especially, which has, so to speak, a vested interest in theology; yet it is, perhaps, a measure of the layman's ignorance and indifference, in matters of religion, that he should be surprised and even shocked to find there are Christians who consider dogma and ritual more vital to their religion than freedom from want and exploitation. T. S. Eliot's *The Idea of a Christian Society*, a palmary exposition of the case for a new hierarchy, is coldly theological and may have been deliberately conceived to offset the vulgar error of those who regard religion as merely a kind of extension, in the realm of the spirit, of the principles of bodily well-being. The same uncompromising intellectualism runs through the seventeen essays, contributed by Anglo-Catholic apologists, to the symposium *Prospect for Christendom*. Their attitude, in so far as it is typical of contemporary Christian ideology, suggests that religious communion in the future may become, like art, the mystery of a privileged class or oligarchy.

On the other hand, there are stronger grounds for supposing that reaction to the present mood of spiritual frustration and to the general disintegration of morality may take the form of a popular revivalist movement. If it should, it is unlikely to originate in those empty churches where, in desperation, some vicars and curates have been driven to offer such inducements as films and dance-music, or parking space for perambulators and dogs, in order to tempt people to come in from the highways and hedges. Nor is it likely to spring from the transcendental teaching of those expatriate British writers, Aldous Huxley, Gerald Heard, and Christopher Isherwood, whose personal cult of a form of neo-Brahminism, involving contemplation and detachment from the world, is a good deal easier to preach and practise on the sunny hillsides of the Golden West than in Britain's grey industrial North.

The enormous sales of *The Screwtape Letters*—a cunning re-statement of Christian doctrine in the form of a witty, not to say facetious, allegory by C. S. Lewis, the Oxford scholar—indicate that there are potentialities in his brand of popular evangelism. Lewis is a skilled dialectician and has a trick of making Christian morality seem attractive, or, at least, as alluring as the modern equivalent of antinomianism. A single tract for the times, however, hardly makes a religious revival, and this best-seller is more likely to make people keep out of the way of the Devil than to show them the way to God.

An approach to God, not by the straight path of religion but by the round-about road of philosophy, was marked out by the popular philosopher, C. E. M. Joad, in his book *God and Evil*. His hold on the multitude is considerable, for, as the most imposing member of the B.B.C.'s "Brains Trust", he has acquired a vast audience for his extemporary and oracular pronouncements on life; and, in doing so, he must have extended the circulation of his books to many people who, while they may not be capable of thinking deeply, are nevertheless prone to the blank misgivings of the creature and grateful for any lightening of their darkness. Dr. Joad's discovery, in late middle-age, that there are, after all, intimations, which even he cannot rationalise away, of a divine purpose in the universe, is unlikely to revive religious practice, though it may help to restore religious belief. Even a vague theism, such as he now publicly affects, might assist others to recover faith in themselves and in their ultimate destiny. Atomic force is no substitute for faith where there are mountains to be removed from the road that should bring man nearer God.

In an age of disbelief, when social security is considered a more momentous issue than spiritual salvation, it is not surprising that man's relation to society has proved to be a more profitable subject for investigation than the individual's relationship with God. It is treated with academic complexity in the late Professor Collingwood's *The New Leviathan*; with a consultant physician's magisterial vagueness in Dr. Kenneth Walker's *Diagnosis of Man*; with Christian feeling and hope in Michael Roberts's anti-Spenglerian *The Recovery of the West*; and with profound religious conviction and philosophic understanding in Karl Mannheim's *Man and Society*. It is a subject which is bound to receive increasing attention during the tedious process of post-war readjustment: in Great Britain, especially, while the Labour Government's programme of " socialisation " is being carried out. Whether it is one that will contribute directly or indirectly to literature remains to be seen. That even an official " White Book " can possess literary merit of a high order, in addition to fulfilling its technical purpose, may have surprised the curious who read the Scott Report on *The Utilization of Land in Rural Areas*. As far as literature is concerned, however, it is a subject which has greater possibilities for the novelist than the sociologist. This has already been shown in the U.S.A., in novels like *The Grapes of Wrath*, in a shift of emphasis from personal to social relationships.

The literature of science, if indeed it has any longer a right, other than *pro forma*, to this title, was curtailed, during the war, by the operation of the Official Secrets Act, which prohibited any writing, except in the most general terms, about recent scientific developments. Furthermore, scientists like J. D. Bernal and C. H. Waddington (author of *The Scientific Attitude* in the " Penguin Books "), who before the war had written about their work with a deep sense of social responsibility, were too heavily engaged in " scientific warfare " to have leisure for writing books. Sir James Jeans, however, continuing his task of making the mysterious Universe appear slightly less incomprehensible to sublunary minds, provided, in *Physics and Philosophy*, a moment's relief for the thoughtful, by diverting attention from themselves to their stars, and by hinting that there are, conceivably, more things in heaven and earth than are dreamt of in contemporary science. Undoubtedly the most important single contribution to scientific " literature " published during the war was Dr. Julian Huxley's *Evolution: the Modern Synthesis*, a masterly systemisation of research and progress made in this department of biology since the death of his grandfather T. H. Huxley. More books of similar scope and distinction are needed, not to " popularise " science, which has been sufficiently vulgarised for the common reader in recent years, but to enable intelligent people to form some general idea both of the implications of scientific research and of the scientific attitude to life. The " Genius of Science " has yet to find, as the " Genius of Christianity " did, its Chateaubriand, and the synoptic gospels of modern Science have yet to be written. Meanwhile, it is in the highest degree desirable that the public should be disabused of the notion that science, whether pure or applied, is merely another word for technology; and that its purpose is dutifully to develop and supply " modern conveniences ", whether in the form of atomic bombs and radiolocation for the General Staff or of television and nylon stockings for the housewife. It is as well to remember that among the more alarming possibilities of misapplied science is the mass production of the moron.

While scientific research proceeded on an ever-increasing scale throughout the war, literary research was brought almost to a standstill. Scholarship, indeed, was more adversely affected by the war than any other branch of literature. The obstacles mentioned at the beginning of this survey, which hampered every kind of literary pursuit in war-time, were peculiarly obstructive to scholarly undertakings. In particular, the inaccessibility of material made it virtually impossible for British scholars to carry on their work. If they were unable to examine rare books and manuscripts, dispersed and hidden away for safety while the war lasted, or procure, except with great difficulty, photostat copies of them from overseas, they were also unable to confer with their colleagues abroad, and at times even with those at home. Direct access to the resources of continental Europe was wholly denied to them. But for the fact that much of their work was already far advanced before the outbreak of war, it is doubtful whether any of it would have been fit for publication before the armistice. It is all the more satisfactory to be able to record even a few such achievements as the first volume of Dr. W. W. Greg's great bibliographical *Catalogue of English Plays*; Professor E. de Selincourt's editions of Dorothy Wordsworth's *Journal* and her brother's early poems; W. Graham's collected edition of the *Letters of Joseph Addison*; the first three volumes by various hands of a new annotated text of Pope's *Poems*; and the addition of several volumes to Professor Herbert Davis's edition of the *Prose Works* of Swift. Here, also, should be mentioned, though they might as well have been referred to under the heading of criticism, two major works of classical scholarship: Dr. C. M. Bowra's *Sophoclean Tragedy*, and the first volume of Dr. W. A. Gomme's *Historical Commentary on Thucydides*. It is worth adding, by way of conclusion, that there was no decline, at any time during the war, in the high quality of the occasional contributions by scholars to such learned periodicals as *The Library*, *The Review of English Studies*, and *The Classical Review*. As much may be said, in commendation, of the papers contributed by specialists, as opportunity served, to those journals devoted to the interests of theology, philosophy, and science.

VII. CONCLUSION

In retrospect, the period under review would seem to a casual observer to have been one of continuous activity, maintained successfully in the face of formidable impediments and in conditions of adversity unprecedented in the annals of authorship. The sternest critic would certainly allow some credit for the fact that so much was written and published in such circumstances. Criticism, however, is not concerned with mere quantity; its standards of value are qualitative, and by these it must finally decide the claim of any piece of writing to literary honours. Such a claim, it must

Dr. C. E. M. Joad: Everyman's Philosopher

C. S. Lewis: Everyman's Moralist

John Lehmann: publisher, editor, poet, critic

Arthur Bryant, John Masefield, O.M., G. M. Trevelyan, O.M., at the Headquarters
of the National Book League

be admitted, cannot be made for the bulk of the books produced in Great Britain between 1939 and 1945. Even discounting the trash and purely topical stuff, published as a commercial speculation, most of it was just unpretentious " reading matter " produced for those who wanted information, technical knowledge, entertainment, or pleasant day-dreams. Only a few of those many thousands of books could be said to satisfy, in form as well as content, the essential prerequisites of literature. Only in these few does one find that fusion of contemporary thought and sensibility which, when perfectly cast in words, shows " the very age and body of the time his form and pressure ". This, it need hardly be said, should not be taken to mean that the period under review was abnormally deficient in this respect. Much less should it be supposed that there is anything unusual in the fact that no great masterpieces were turned out in a short space of six years.

Yet, disregard for the formal principles of literary expression is, perhaps, inevitable when few people care whether a book is well written or not, and fewer still are capable of appreciating the difference. It is enough for the great majority of readers nowadays if a writer expresses himself sufficiently well to hold their attention; and most writers are content to do this without troubling themselves with problems of style. Such exceptions as there are to this common practice reveal all too plainly the distinction that now exists between the art of literature and mere communication. This distinction is likely to become even more pronounced if the promoters of Basic English have their way and the use of its verbless vocabulary of a thousand " key " words, as an effective means of communication, becomes at all widespread.

It may be argued that it is useless to expect the nightingale to sing to ears that cannot discriminate between its music and the chattering of starlings; and that it is better to catch the ear of the philistines somehow than not at all. To argue thus is virtually to admit that a writer's business is simply to supply the public demand for " reading matter ". It is an argument which has received indirect but powerful encouragement from the press, the radio, and the cinema. Their influence has been harmful to literature in many ways, not least in its tendency to drive literature into the refuge of a minority. It has often been alleged that the cinema and the radio have created a demand for good books, and that the expansion of the reading public owes much to the mental and emotional excitement they arouse. Yet, how often has it been shown that these books are read, not for their own sake, but because they are, so to speak, the " books of the words " of some film or radio " feature ". It would seem pointless to recommend a method of literary appreciation, such as that advocated by I. A. Richards in *How to Read a Page*, or by L. A. G. Strong in *English for Pleasure*, or by Montgomery Belgion in *Reading for Profit* (written in a German P.O.W. camp), to the great mass of people, who only read to acquire information, or to be told a story, or to confirm and re-capitulate in greater detail something previously seen or heard at the cinema or on the radio.

The growth of literacy and the emergence of a new class of reader have been induced to a large extent by those very forces which, in so far as they cater for the lowest common denominator of public taste, are the enemies of good writing. Respect for literary values is inconsistent with their policy of " giving people what they want ". Yet, if literature is to continue to be a civilising element in society, it must do more than preserve a tradition; it must develop its capacities with the needs of the times and, realising the immense potentialities that exist in this expanding market, must learn how to control it. If it fails in this task it will be reduced to the status of an art pursued for art's sake by isolated groups of writers, segregated from the world in their ivory towers and "private worlds ".

This decline into parochialism is not as yet an immediate danger: but symptoms of it may be detected, perhaps, in the proliferation during the war years of " little reviews " and similar ephemeral organs of an introverted intelligentsia. During those years, how-ever, two periodicals—*Horizon* and *New Writing & Day-Light*, edited respectively by Cyril Connolly and John Lehmann—fought con-sistently against this tendency by maintaining intellectual relations with the Continent, the former chiefly with France, the latter with central Europe and the Balkans. Without these slender links with continental thought a vital and vitalising source of strength might well have been lost to English literature for many years to come. For all the apparent insularity of the British people, their literary culture is indiscerptibly rooted in the European tradition and, if it is to flourish in the future, it is essential for these ties to be strengthened and multiplied. Those who have lately condemned, not to say ridiculed, an excess of Francophily in certain quarters would be better occupied in diagnosing its causes, which lie deep in the common origins of Western civilisation.

If literature is to extend its civilising mission among the literate masses; if it is not to become the arcane cult of a mandarin class; it must impose its values, and insist on their supreme importance, no matter what the odds are against their easy acceptance. These odds may now seem heavy indeed, for the counter-attraction of working for the press, the cinema, the radio, and the purveyors of commercialised " reading matter ", offers itself to any writer who is willing to prostitute himself to their public. Newspaper barons and film magnates have shown that it is not difficult to bend authors to their own desires; and the radio, if it does not actually dictate, exercises a subtle control over the ideas of its script-writers. These insidious corruptors of an artist's integrity are destructive of literary values. Resistance to them must come from within, the writer himself creating the anti-bodies to protect his integrity.

This is not to say that literature must become " engaged ", as one school of continental writers now insists; that it must, in other words, " take sides " in the social revolution, if it is to continue to express and to record the drama of the human condition. There was enough of this kind of polemical writing in Britain during the 1930's to show that it is not on public platforms any more than in ivory towers that literature prospers. The integrity of the individual writer can best be defended from all the forces currently arrayed against it, by an attitude of absolute intransigence towards the philistine and all his works. Not only in the immediate post-war era but during the years of man's painful spiritual recovery which lie ahead, such an attitude must be preserved if, out of disintegration, a scheme of values is to arise and out of disillusionment a dynamic faith in the power of the printed word to express the finest operations of human thought and sensibility.

SELECT BIBLIOGRAPHY

I. WAR BOOKS

1940–1941—Lord Chatfield: *The Navy and Defence*. Winston S. Churchill: *Into Battle* (Speeches). A. Duff Cooper: *The Second World War*. Cyril Falls: *The Nature of Modern Warfare*. E. M. Forster: *Nordic Twilight*. David Garnett: *War in the Air*. Philip Gibbs: *The Amazing Summer*. Nevile Henderson: *Failure of a Mission*. John Pope-Hennessy: *History under Fire*. Inez Holden: *Night Shift*. Julian Huxley: *Democracy Marches*. Collie Knox: *Atlantic Battle*. Arthur Koestler: *Scum of the Earth, Darkness at Noon*. Eric Linklater: *The Cornerstones*. Lord Lothian: *American Speeches*. John Masefield: *The Nine Days' Wonder*. David Masters: *So Few*. Ministry of Information: *The Battle of Britain, Bomber Command*. Elinor Mordaunt: *Blitz Kids*. Dilys Powell: *Remember Greece*. George Schuster and Guy Wint: *India and Democracy*. J. M. Spaight: *The Battle of Britain*. John Strachey: *Post D*. Leo Walmsley: *Fishermen at War*.

1942—B.B.C.: *Calling All Nations*. Cecil Beaton: *Winged Squadrons*. Alan Brodrick: *North Africa*. Stanley Casson: *Greece Against the Axis*. Winston S. Churchill: *The Unrelenting Struggle* (Speeches). D. M. Crook: *Spitfire Pilot*. J. F. C. Fuller: *Machine Warfare*. Philip Guedalla: *The Liberators*. B. H. Liddell Hart: *This Expanding War, The British Way in Warfare*. Richard Hillary: *The Last Enemy*. Gordon Holman: *Commando Attack*. E. F. Jacob (Editor): *What We Defend*. David Masters: *Up Periscope*. Ministry of Information: *The Campaign in Greece and Crete, The Abyssinian Campaigns, The Saga of San Demetrio, Ark Royal, The Highland Division, Transport Goes to War, Front Line, 1940–41*, etc. M. A. Sargeaunt and Geoffrey West: *Grand Strategy*. G. L. Steer: *Sealed and Delivered, When We Build Again*. Derek Tangye (Editor): *Went the Day Well*. Brian Tunstall: *The World War at Sea*. Alexander Werth: *Moscow '41*. Flying Officer " X " (H. E. Bates): *The Greatest People in the World*.

1943—A. B. Austin: *We Landed at Dawn*. Hector Bolitho: *Combat Report: The Story of a Fighter Pilot*. Winston S. Churchill: *The End of the Beginning* (Speeches). Alexander Clifford: *Three Against Rommel*. Cyril Falls: *Ordeal by Battle*. C. S. Forester: *The Ship* (novel). Margaret Goldsmith: *Women at War*. E. Tangye Lean:

Voices in the Darkness. Compton Mackenzie: *Wind of Freedom.* David Masters: *With Pennants Flying.* F. O. Miksche: *Paratroops.* Ministry of Information: *Fleet Air Arm, Northern Garrisons, Coastal Command, Roof Over Britain, His Majesty's Minesweepers, Combined Operations, 1940–42,* etc. Alan Moorehead: *The End in Africa.* Ian Morrison: *This War Against Japan.* A. C. Pigou: *The Transition from War to Peace.* J. B. Priestley: *British Women go to War.* George Rodger: *Red Moon Rising.* Owen Rutter: *Red Ensign.* Amabel Williams-Ellis: *Women in War Factories.*

1944—Winston S. Churchill: *Onwards to Victory* (Speeches). Philip Guedalla: *Middle East, 1940–42.* David Halley: *With Wingate in Burma.* Joseph Kessel: *Army of Shadows.* R. B. McCallum: *England and France.* Ministry of Information: *The Mediterranean Fleet, The Air Battle of Malta, The Royal Marines.* Alan Moorehead: *African Trilogy.* Hilary St. George Saunders: *Per Ardua.* Godfrey Talbot: *Speaking from the Desert.* Alexander Werth: *Leningrad.* H. A. Wyndham: *Britain and the World.*

1945—Winston S. Churchill: *The Dawn of Liberation* (Speeches). Richard Dimbleby: *The Waiting Year.* R. C. K. Ensor: *A Miniature History of the War Down to the Liberation of Paris.* Bernard Fergusson: *Beyond the Chindwin.* Simon Harcourt-Smith: *The Fate of Japan.* George Millar: *Maquis.* Ministry of Information: *Arctic War, Atlantic Bridge, Merchantmen at War, His Majesty's Submarines, By Air to Battle.* Alan Moorehead: *Eclipse.* W. B. Kennedy Shaw: *Long Range Desert Group.* Stephen Spender: *Citizens in War.* Flora Stark (Editor): *An Italian Diary.* J. E. Taylor: *Northern Escort.* Anonymous: *Arnhem Lift : The Diary of a Glider Pilot.*

1946—Winston S. Churchill: *Victory* (Speeches), *Secret Session Speeches.* General Dwight D. Eisenhower: *Report by the Supreme Commander to the Combined Chiefs of Staff on the Operations in Europe of the Allied Expeditionary Forces : 6 June 1944 to 8 May 1945.* Field-Marshal The Viscount Montgomery of Alamein: *Operations in North-West Europe from 6 June 1944 to 5 May 1945;* and other Reports.

GENERAL—*Hutchinson's Quarterly Record of the War* (Ronald Storrs: *The First Quarter, The Second Quarter;* Philip Graves: *The Third Quarter to The Twenty-Second Quarter*—2 further volumes in preparation). Edgar McInnis: *The War : First Year, The War : Second Year, The War : Third Year, The War : Fourth Year, The War : Fifth Year.* "Strategicus": *The War for World Power, From Tobruk to Smolensk, The War Moves East, From Dunkirk to Benghazi, To Stalingrad and Alamein, The Tide Turns, Foothold in Europe.*

D

2. BIOGRAPHY AND AUTOBIOGRAPHY

William D'Arfey: *Curious Relations*. Thomas Beecham: *A Mingled Chime*. Lord Berners: *A Distant Prospect*. Elizabeth Bowen: *Bowen's Court*. John Buchan: *Memory Hold-the-Door*. Algernon Cecil: *A House in Bryanston Square, Metternich*. Cyril Connolly (" Palinurus "): *The Unquiet Grave*. G. G. Coulton: *Fourscore Years*. Guy Eden: *Portrait of Churchill*. E. M. Forster: *Virginia Woolf* (Rede Lecture). Eric Gill: *Autobiography*. T. R. Glover: *Cambridge Retrospect*. George S. Gordon: *Letters*. Herbert Gorman: *James Joyce*. A. S. F. Gow: *Letters from Cambridge, 1939–44*. G. B. Grundy: *55 Years at Oxford*. Philip Guedalla: *The Two Marshals*. G. H. Hardy: *A Mathematician's Apology*. Una Pope-Hennessy: *Charles Dickens*. H. Hensley Henson: *Retrospect of an Unimportant Life*. James Hone: *W. B. Yeats, 1865–1939*. Joseph Hone (Editor): *J. B. Yeats: Letters to his Son, W. B. Yeats and Others*. Aldous Huxley: *Grey Eminence*. L. P. Jacks: *The Confession of an Octogenarian*. Marie Belloc Lowndes: *" I, Too, Have Lived in Arcadia", Where Love and Friendship Dwelt*. C. M. Maclean: *Born Under Saturn* (Hazlitt). John Masefield: *In the Mill, New Chum*. Sarah Gertrude Millin: *The Night is Long*. Sean O'Casey: *I Knock at the Door, Pictures in the Hallway, Drums Under the Windows*. Charles Oman: *Memories of Victorian Oxford*. F. D. Ommanney: *The House in the Park*. Hesketh Pearson: *Bernard Shaw*. William Plomer: *Double Lives*. Lord Ponsonby : *Henry Ponsonby*. Peter Quennell: *Byron in Italy, Four Portraits*. Herbert Read: *Annals of Innocence and Experience*. Forrest Reid: *Private Road*. Denys Reitz: *Commando, Trekking on, No Outspan*. Grant Richards: *Housman: 1897–1936*. V. Sackville-West: *The Eagle and the Dove*. Siegfried Sassoon: *The Weald of Youth, Siegfried's Journey*. Jack Simmons: *Southey*. Osbert Sitwell: *Left Hand, Right Hand!* Enid Starkie: *A Lady's Child*. C. V. Wedgwood: *William the Silent*. Denton Welch: *Maiden Voyage, In Youth is Pleasure*. E. L. Woodward: *Short Journey*. Virginia Woolf: *Roger Fry*.

3. ESSAYS AND CRITICISM

Montgomery Belgion: *Reading for Profit*. Joan Bennett: *Virginia Woolf, Her Art as a Novelist*. Elizabeth Bowen: *English Novelists*. Maurice Bowra: *The Heritage of Symbolism, From Virgil to Milton, Sophoclean Tragedy*. Lord David Cecil: *Hardy the Novelist* (Clark Lectures).

Cyril Connolly: *The Condemned Playground*. Alan Dent: *Preludes and Studies*. David Douglas: *English Scholars*. T. S. Eliot: *What is a Classic?*, *The Classics and the Man of Letters; Addresses in Paris, Stockholm, etc.* (unpublished). William Gaunt: *The Pre-Raphaelite Tragedy, The Aesthetic Adventure*. T. R. Glover: *Springs of Hellas and other Essays*. Herbert Grierson: *Essays and Addresses, A Critical History of English Poetry* (with J. C. Smith). Humphry House: *The Dickens World*. Wilson Knight: *Chariot of Wrath, The Olive and the Sword*. Constant Lambert: *Music Ho!* C. S. Lewis: *A Preface to "Paradise Lost", Hamlet: The Prince or the Poem?* (British Academy Lecture), *Clark Lectures* (unpublished). Robert Lynd: *Things One Hears*. Louis MacNeice: *The Poetry of W. B. Yeats*. Charles Morgan: *Reflections in a Mirror*. Raymond Mortimer: *Channel Packet, Clark Lectures* (unpublished). George Orwell: *Critical Essays*. V. S. Pritchett: *In My Good Books*. Herbert Read: *Education through Art, A Coat of Many Colours*. Forrest Reid: *Retrospective Adventures*. I. A. Richards: *How to Read a Page*. A. L. Rowse: *The English Spirit*. Denis Saurat: *Milton, Man and Thinker*. Francis Scarfe: *Auden and After*. Edith Sitwell: *A Poet's Notebook*. Osbert Sitwell: *Sing High! Sing Low!, A Letter to My Son*. Sacheverell Sitwell: *Sacred and Profane Love, Splendours and Miseries, Primitive Scenes and Festivals, British Architects and Craftsmen*. J. C. Smith: *A Study of Wordsworth*. Logan Pearsall Smith: *Milton and his Modern Critics*. Stephen Spender: *Life and the Poet*. Adrian Stokes: *Venice: An Aspect of Art*. L. A. G. Strong: *English for Pleasure* (Broadcast Talks). Geoffrey Tillotson: *Essays in Criticism and Research*. E. M. W. Tillyard: *The Elizabethan World Picture, Shakespeare's History Plays*. L. P. Wilkinson: *Horace and his Lyric Poetry*. Basil Willey: *The Eighteenth Century Background*. Charles Williams: *Figure of Beatrice, Introduction to English Poems of John Milton* (World's Classics). J. Dover Wilson: *The Fortunes of Falstaff* (Clark Lectures). Virginia Woolf: *The Death of the Moth and other Essays*. G. M. Young: *Essays and Reviews* (unpublished).

4. HISTORY, POLITICS AND TRAVEL

Ernest Barker: *Reflections on Government*. Cecil Beaton and Peter Quennell: *Time Exposure* (enlarged edition, 1946). William Beveridge: *Social Insurance and Allied Services* (The "Beveridge Report"), *Full Employment in a Free Society, Price of Peace*. D. W. Brogan: *The Development of Modern France, The English People, The American Problem*. Arthur Bryant: *Unfinished Victory, English Saga (1840–1940), The*

Years of Endurance (1793–1802), *Years of Victory* (1802–1814).
Harold Butler: *The Lost Peace: A Personal Impression*. E. H. Carr:
Conditions of Peace. John Clapham: *The Bank of England: A History*.
R. Coupland: *The Future of India*. Lindley Fraser: *Germany Between
Two Wars*. W. A. Gomme: *A Historical Commentary on Thucydides*.
G. P. Gooch: *Studies in Diplomacy and Statecraft*. Robert Graves and
Alan Hodge: *The Long Week-end* (1918–39). Harold Laski: *Reflec-
tions on the Revolution of our Time*. A. D. Lindsay: *The Modern Demo-
cratic State*. J. T. MacCurdy: *Germany, Russia, and the Future*.
Pierre Maillaud: *The English Way*. David Mathew: *Naval Heritage*.
Charles Morgan: *The House of Macmillan, 1843–1943*. L. B. Namier:
Conflicts: Studies in Contemporary History. P. Nathan: *The Psychology
of Fascism*. Carola Oman: *Britain Against Napoleon*. Bernard Pares:
Russia. Herbert Read: *The Politics of the Unpolitical*. H.M.S.O.
Publications: *Scott Report, Uthwatt Report*, etc. B. Seebohm Rown-
tree: *Poverty and Progress: A Second Social Survey of York*. A. L.
Rowse: *Tudor Cornwall, The Spirit of English History*. Freya Stark:
The Southern Gates of Arabia, The Valleys of the Assassins, East is West.
G. M. Trevelyan: *English Social History, Trinity College: An Historical
Sketch*. F. A. Voigt: *Pax Britannica*. F. Kingdon Ward: *Modern
Exploration, Assam Adventure*. Rebecca West: *Black Lamb and Grey
Falcon*.

5. RELIGION, PHILOSOPHY, SCIENCE, ETC.

E. B. Balfour: *Living Soil*. K. Barlow: *The Discipline of Peace*. F. W. Bate-
son (editor): *The Cambridge Bibliography of English Literature*.[1]
A. C. F. Beales: *The Catholic Church and International Order*. J. D.
Bernal: *The Social Function of Science* (Jan. 1939). R. G. Colling-
wood: *The New Leviathan*. T. S. Eliot: *The Idea of a Christian Society*.
Michael Graham: *Soil and Sense*. Gerald Heard: *Man the Master,
The Code of Christ, A Preface to Prayer*. H. Hensley Henson: *The
Church of England*. Julian Huxley: *Evolution, On Living in a Revolu-
tion: Fifteen Essays*. James Jeans: *Physics and Philosophy*. C. E. M.
Joad: *Philosophy for our Times, God and Evil*. Ronald Knox: *God and
the Atom*. John Laird: *Mind and Deity* (Gifford Lectures). C. S.
Lewis: *The Screwtape Letters*. Karl Mannheim: *Man and Society*.
Lord Moran: *The Anatomy of Courage*. Leslie Paul: *The Annihilation
of Man*. M. B. Reckitt (Editor): *Prospect for Christendom* (*Anglo-
Catholic Symposium*). Michael Roberts: *The Recovery of the West*.

---

[1] This great work of reference, though published in 1940, was completed
before the war.

Bertrand Russell: *The Conquest of Happiness, An Inquiry into Meaning and Truth.* John Russell: *Agriculture Today and Tomorrow, English Farming.* William Temple: *Christianity and the Social Order, Malvern 1941 (The Malvern Conference), Malvern and After.* C. H. Waddington: *The Scientific Attitude.* Kenneth Walker: *Diagnosis of Man.* H. G. Wells: *The Fate of Homo Sapiens.* Charles Williams: *Witchcraft.* P. H. Winfield: *The Foundations and Future of International Law.*

British Book News, *a monthly classified and annotated selection of recent books on all subjects published in Britain, can be obtained free by residents outside the United Kingdom on application to the* National Book League, 7 Albemarle Street, London, W.1.

THE NOVEL SINCE 1939

Henry Reed himself belongs to the generation of young writers who have become known since 1939. While in the Army, and, later, in the Foreign Office, he has written poetry and criticism that have already earned for him a high reputation. He is a regular contributor to *The Listener*, *New Writing* and other literary periodicals, and has for some time been Novel critic of the *New Statesman*. He has recently published his first volume of poems, *A Map of Verona*.

This essay, therefore, may be taken as representing the reactions of a sensitive and intelligent young critic to the work of British novelists during the war years.

Uniform with this Volume

THE ARTS IN BRITAIN

JAMES JOYCE

THE NOVEL SINCE 1939

By

HENRY REED

Illustrated

Published for

THE BRITISH COUNCIL

by LONGMANS GREEN & CO

LONDON   NEW YORK   TORONTO

LONGMANS, GREEN AND CO. LTD.
OF PATERNOSTER ROW
43 ALBERT DRIVE, LONDON, S.W.19
NICOL ROAD, BOMBAY
17 CHITTARANJAN AVENUE, CALCUTTA
36A MOUNT ROAD, MADRAS

LONGMANS, GREEN AND CO.
55 FIFTH AVENUE, NEW YORK, 3

LONGMANS, GREEN AND CO.
215 VICTORIA STREET, TORONTO, 1

LONGMANS' CODE NUMBER : 10035 (English)

THIS BOOKLET IS PRODUCED IN
COMPLETE CONFORMITY WITH THE
AUTHORISED ECONOMY STANDARDS

C

BRITISH COUNCIL'S CODE NAME : NOVEL (ENGLISH)

First published 1946

SET IN MONOTYPE PERPETUA
DESIGNED BY ERIC GILL

PRINTED IN GREAT BRITAIN
BY R. & R. CLARK, LIMITED, EDINBURGH

ILLUSTRATIONS

The opinions expressed in this book are the author's, and not necessarily those of the British Council.

THE NOVEL SINCE 1939

IN the following pages I attempt, as fairly as I can, to give a brief picture of how one English reader regards the landscape of the contemporary English novel; allowances must therefore be made for personal idiosyncrasy of taste and judgement. I cannot lay claim to impartiality, and in case the reader forget this, I shall perhaps use the reminders "I think" and "it seems to me" rather more often than would be normally tolerable. I have written as an intellectual addressing other intellectuals; and one tract of contemporary fiction I have therefore omitted: the best-sellers, even the more refined and sophisticated ones, which everyone has ample opportunity of judging for himself. I am concerned here with the fate of the novel at the hands of the serious practitioner as distinct from the writer who cavalierly uses the novel for the distillation of political or philosophical ideas. Some sort of philosophy or view of life, often with political implications, inevitably emerges from the work of a serious novelist; but it *emerges*; it does not insert itself, or stand there for the novel to drape itself round. The true novelist is one enthralled by his chosen form, deeply respectful of it, and consistently curious about what new depths it enables him to penetrate. I have ignored also those writers for whom tradition is simply a guide towards something to imitate. These writers are, alas, the writers who most easily get exported, and it is partly to dissuade the foreign reader from exclusive attention to them that these pages have been written. It is the novelist who will not easily come his way, and who nevertheless seems, to an English reader, significant or full of promise, that I wish to discuss and to place in what I judge to be a perspective.

I have been asked to deal principally with the novel since 1939. But since one cannot pretend that the contemporary novel *began* in 1939, I have first tried to give some indication of what is at the back of our minds in England when we read a new novel of importance: some indication, that is to say, of what our terms of reference are, so far as the immediate past is concerned, and of how the novel of today joins on to the novel of the past. And in my concluding paragraphs, since a mere six-year cross-section would force one to ignore significant writers who have for various reasons written very little during that time, I have mentioned some writers whose voices, now that the war is over, may be expected to rejoin those who have contrived to remain moderately prolific.

It will be noticed that I have given most of my space to a fairly detailed account of half a dozen outstanding writers. These again are a personal choice, though I believe that most fiction critics in England today would not violently dissent from it. But I have dwelt on them principally because one approaches a phase of literature through its best individual writers, and usually through a small number of them. The writers in the body of this essay are highly individualised, and wholly distinct from each other; it is easier to begin with them than with any discussion of " tendencies ". The latter, in fact, would be beyond my powers to describe, even if I were at all convinced that they existed.

I

Revivals and temporary burials of literary figures are always taking place. No-one in war-time England could fail to observe that, after forty years of comparative neglect, Anthony Trollope has regained some of the enormous popularity he enjoyed in his own day; or that, after a short eclipse, Joseph Conrad is beginning to revive; or that D. H. Lawrence is, for the moment, all but forgotten. One would like to discourse on these writers; but there are three others from the immediate past who more decisively claim our attention as forming part of the background of the contemporary novel.

First, there is Thomas Hardy. It is nineteen years since Hardy died, and the last thirty years of his life were devoted not to the novel but to poetry. But neither as poet nor as novelist has he suffered that temporary eclipse which so many writers suffer soon after their death. Quite apart from his unshakeable achievement, he remains important because of the tragic breadth he brought into the novel, because of his sense of design, and above all because of the strong poetic element in his novels. He had no wish to write novels; he wrote his novels in order to make a living, and for a quarter of a century his poetry had to be relegated to the fugitive moments of his time. But he was never less than a poet: and the lyrical quality which pervades the atmosphere, the setting and even the character-drawing of his novels, is what gives him his particular and original glory. His sense of form and his poetry have greatly affected the English novel, even in writers who share nothing of his tragic sense; and his outspokenness about love and marriage in his later novels has likewise affected succeeding generations.

The second figure is Henry James, who has entered on a period of popularity which he never attained in his lifetime. Indeed, during the latter part of his life, his number of readers was infinitesimal. His present popularity is only partly explained by the fact that 1943 was the anniversary of his birth, or by the fact that the indoor qualities of his prose, the slow motion of his plots (and beneath all the words there always *is* a plot, often highly melodramatic) have been a refuge from the violence of the " real " world. The revival is more than that. It is among writers that these resuscitations begin, and James has never been neglected by his fellow-craftsmen. (He is popularly known as The Master.) It is not difficult to see what has attracted them. First there is his habit of complicating his problems, complicating them for the profound aesthetic pleasure of solving them; the title of his most popular story, *The Turn of the Screw*, refers, as much as to anything, to the successive twists he gave to his angle of vision and attitude before starting on the story. He is one of the most selfless of artists, and his wonderful prefaces to the collected edition of his novels are a mine of information about artistic processes. Secondly, there is his attitude to language, implicit in the intricate sentences he uses. Only lavish quotations could demonstrate the subtlety of his extraordinary prose, his complete awareness of what he wants to convey, his peculiar use of tiny clichés as a kind of central jewel to an elaborately-wrought sentence. Yet even when his design and his language have been acknowledged, quite half of James has been left out: the sensibility of which these are the expression, the horror and disgust, the great sense of evil and of " the black and merciless things that are behind great possessions ". And it is these latter things that have most struck the younger writers who have admired him; through all the apparent obfuscations of his prose, his prodigious moral sense shines clearly. And somehow the prose is finally part of the light.

YVK   The third figure is James Joyce, who died in Zurich in 1941, not long after the publication of *Finnegans Wake*, which is the crown of a lifetime's work. The two most important earlier works of Joyce are *A Portrait of the Artist as a Young Man* and *Ulysses*, both too well known throughout the world to need comment here; indeed for fifteen years *Ulysses* was better known outside the United Kingdom than in. *Finnegans Wake*, however, demands so complete a consciousness of the linguistic norm—English—from which it departs that it is inconceivable that it will ever be widely read outside the British Empire and America; and perhaps never widely read there, for years of at least intermittent attention are required for its mastering: yet even a superficial acquaintance with its intention and design, and an habituation to its linguistic method (not difficult to acquire), are enough to reveal its stupendous greatness as a work of art. *Ulysses* dealt in a variety of " techniques " with a day's waking life; *Finnegans Wake* deals with a night's sleeping life. But sleep embraces more than waking; and a whole history of the world accretes itself to the dreams of H. C. E. in *Finnegans Wake*. The language in which Joyce chooses to express this vast dream is distorted with heavy associations in the manner of Carroll's nonsense poem *Jabberwocky*. It is an exhausting work to read, but immeasurably rewarding.

There are many things to be said about Joyce: he is important to these pages for two particular reasons. First, the publication during the war of a part (pages 519–902) of *Stephen Hero*, the early version of *A Portrait of the Artist*, written apparently while Joyce was between the ages of nineteen and twenty-four. Joyce seems to have destroyed the rest of the manuscript, and in later years he referred to it as a "schoolboy's production". Compared with the final *Portrait*, with its marvellous evolutionary style, perhaps it is; yet it has infinitely more power than much that one commonly regards as mature. There are wonderful passages of dialogue, ruthlessly condensed or rejected in the final work, which are a great delight to possess. Indeed these dialogues are the outstanding characteristic of the earlier work. It is clear, however, that *Stephen Hero* (whatever the character of that part of it now lost) cannot have been a work of art that would satisfy its exacting creator; it must certainly have lacked compulsion, rhythm and conclusiveness. For the present-day reader, that is part of its interest. The unforgettable beauty of the *Portrait* is always with one as one reads *Stephen Hero*; the collocation of the two shows simultaneously both the stress of a great creative mind preparing for action, and the superbity of its final decisions, rejections and achievements.

Finally, it must be remembered that Joyce's *Ulysses* has a central importance in English fiction today. (It has been described as the novel to end novels, and there is a little truth in the description. When Mr. T. S. Eliot, describing Virgil's classic qualities, points out that a great language culminated in the *Aeneid* and was exhausted by it, one is reminded of the way in which *Ulysses* straddles across contemporary fiction.) Its effect on style and technique has been widespread. Little remains to be said about Joyce's employment of the " interior monologue "—though few contemporary writers are unaffected by it. But the prime effect of Joyce's novel is that it has made serious writers more conscious of style and of the necessity of fitting style to matter. The leisurely, mildly ironic stodginess in which so much of the fiction of the century has been written seems dreadfully exposed by Joyce, who recoiled from it with a horror that finds its expression in his frequent parodies. Unfortunately many writers who have recoiled with him have recoiled into the brawny arms of Mr. Ernest Hemingway, whose tough, staccato style has had a catastrophic influence. Joyce is enough to upset any young writer; but he must be recognised as fathering into existence the direct sensitive style which, with individual inflections, many of the best writers of our time use.

II

From Hardy our novelists inherit a legacy of poetry and architecture; from James a legacy of subtlety and psychological curiosity; from Joyce a rejuvenation of language. And from all three, many other things as well. They are giants among writers. But there are two other writers, working on a much smaller scale, who also form part of the background: E. M. Forster and Virginia Woolf. E. M. Forster is still alive, but has written no novels for twenty-two years. His best novel, *A Passage to India*, was published in 1924; the novel which preceded that, *Howards End*, was written eleven years earlier. His works have always been particularly dear to his fellow-craftsmen—his influence on younger novelists like Christopher Isherwood, Elizabeth Bowen and William Plomer has been considerable—but not until the second great war have his novels attained a decisively wide popularity. They are always centred on a contrast between a false form of life and a true form, between what he calls the " undeveloped heart " and the open one. They are comic in manner, which makes the sudden intrusion of tragedy more agonising. The perfect clarity of his style, his urbanity and passion, his sensitiveness and comic power, have enabled him to survive the presence of Joyce: he is one of the few writers who immediately preceded Joyce who do survive *Ulysses*. I cannot help feeling that, different as they are, Forster and Joyce share a disgust at clichés—in both life and literature. During the war Forster has seemed a great and distinguished figure, bold, honest and incapable of being hoodwinked. His paper on " The New Disorder "—an affirmation of a belief that only two " orders " are really possible to men, the divine and the artistic—is well worth reading; he is a writer whom one would greatly like to be known in the Europe he himself knows so well.

Virginia Woolf, though she forms part of what I have called the background, carries us right into the foreground. She and Forster were friends and they have written illuminatingly, and with critical determination, about each other's art. Mrs. Woolf died by her own hand in 1941, and three books by her have been posthumously issued; one imagines they are not the last, and she is one of those rare writers whose fugitive or unfinished works the reader is eager to see. *The Death of the Moth* is a collection of essays written with that amazing urbane grace which characterised all her critical writings. *A Haunted House* is a collection of what are best called short stories, though the term is inadequate. All the qualities of Mrs. Woolf's major work are to be found in this little collection: the magical power of observation, the finest sensibility of the age, the loving command of language and rhythm. There are eighteen stories, none of them long, and one or two so brief that they are almost prose-poems. All of them are characterised by that elusiveness which is at the same time in Virginia Woolf's hands a kind of preciseness. Twelve of the stories date from very early collections which have not been reprinted; they vary considerably in manner, according to their date. The remaining six are late work, and four of these are but early drafts. No page lacks its characteristic care, subtlety and distinction, and the book may be read as an introduction to her work as a whole. But it provides no substitute for reading her work in its chronological entirety; and to this the third posthumous volume, *Between the Acts*, 1941, provides a brilliant climax. It is worth while briefly to recall her progress. Her first two novels, *The Voyage Out* and *Night and Day*, do not indicate emphatically any new departure from the traditional forms of the novel. But in 1919 in an essay on contemporary fiction she defined with care her dissatisfaction with the methods of Galsworthy, Bennett and Wells; as presenters of the stuff and feel of life, these writers were not adequate. They omitted, for all their animation, life itself. I must quote at length from this essay, for it is one of those manifestos that have contributed towards a great change in the novel:

Examine for a moment an ordinary mind on an ordinary day. The mind receives a myriad impressions—trivial, fantastic, evanescent, or ingraved with the sharpness of steel. From all sides they come, an incessant shower of innumerable atoms, and as they fall, as they shape themselves into the life of Monday or Tuesday, the accent falls differently from of old; the moment of importance came not here but there; so that, if the writer were a free man and not a slave, if he could write what he chose, not what he must, if he could base his work upon his own feeling and not upon convention, there would be no plot, no comedy, no tragedy, and no love interest or catastrophe in the accepted style. . . . Life is not a series of gig-lamps symmetrically arranged; life is a luminous halo, a semi-transparent envelope surrounding us from the beginning of consciousness to the end. Is it not the task of the novelist to convey this varying, this unknown and uncircumscribed spirit, whatever aberration or complexity it may display?

At the time this essay was being written, *Ulysses* was already appearing serially in *The Little Review*, and there can be no doubt of its influence on *Jacob's Room*, which appeared in the same year, 1922, as the complete version of Joyce's great novel. It is not a long work, though it covers a long period; it is a picture of a young man, built up from fragmentary observations for which the consciousness of others is the principal medium of transmission. It is a striking novel, indeed a landmark, but it remains a collection of fragments, all admirably done, yet not cohering into a whole. *To the Lighthouse* and *Mrs. Dalloway* contrive to impose a poetic or musical form on the material. *To the Lighthouse*, indeed, which is divided into sections which reflect the *flash*, *dark*, *flash* of the lighthouse itself, does in its shape recall some of Joyce's devices. To these books succeed *The Waves*, which is often assumed to be Mrs. Woolf's masterpiece, and *The Years*, a more " normal " novel with which most readers have been disappointed.

Between the Acts, unrevised as it is, seems to me to be her finest work. It is succinct, and yet it has an enormous range; the occasional preciosity and fussiness, which attend some of the very best of her earlier works, do not intrude here. The book occupies only a brief space of time—it centres on a performance of a pageant of English history on the lawn of a country house. At its core, between the acts of the pageant and between the acts of history, (the two great wars), is the agony of a present moment, a domestic flaw in the relations of Isa and her husband; around it spread our crude ideas of history, and beyond that our vague ideas of prehistory. The whole is bound together with a strength which its

Virginia Woolf

E. M. FORSTER

gentleness at all times disguises. From *To the Lighthouse* onwards this has perhaps always been so, yet Mrs. Woolf's strength has sometimes seemed to be camouflaged more than has really been necessary. Here it is not so. One may quote its final sentences as a perfect example of her art at those points where it touches greatness, and where her curious tragic sense reveals itself most clearly. At the end of the day Isa and her husband Giles are left alone together:

Left alone together for the first time that day, they were silent. Alone enmity was bared; also love. Before they slept, they must fight; after they had fought, they would embrace. From that embrace another life might be born. But first they must fight, as the dog fights with the vixen, in the heart of darkness, in the fields of night.

Isa let her sewing drop. The great hooded chairs had become enormous. And Giles too. And Isa too against the window. The window was all sky without colour. The house had lost its shelter. It was night before roads were made, or houses. It was the night that dwellers in caves had watched from some high place among rocks.

Then the curtain rose. They spoke.

III

Despite their insight and their honesty, Forster and Mrs. Woolf have somewhere, deep down, a kind of sentimentality which may not greatly mar their work, but which does diminish it a little. So that turning from them to the three novelists I next have to consider is almost like returning to a centre from which Forster and Mrs. Woolf have—quite conscientiously—strayed. Hardy had a sense of tragic destiny, James had a sense of evil, Joyce had a sense of ineluctable human suffering springing from a " secret cause " which he set himself to reveal. There is nothing so strong as these in Forster and Mrs. Woolf. In the work of two more recent novelists, Graham Greene and I. Compton-Burnett, we get a return to the sense of evil. And in a third, Elizabeth Bowen, we get, what is akin to this, a harrowing impression of the contrast between experience and innocence.

Graham Greene was born in 1905; he is a Roman Catholic by conversion, and his books are deeply affected by this fact. His Catholicism gives him an extra power, and sets him, since he is writing in a non-Catholic country, an extra problem. He has written a considerable number of novels, some of which, lighter in character and in implication than his four or five major works, he calls " entertainments ". His approach to the novel is like that of no novelist in English before him, though he is not without his successors. It is as if he had taken the bones of the conventional thriller, clothed them with life and character, and elevated them to a symbolic purpose; he has in fact seen what is psychologically archetypical in such popular literary themes as that of the hunted man and has dramatised them with all the vigour and consciousness of serious art. He has learnt from popular literature the way of stripping the action of woolliness, and his opening chapters are invariably arresting. One never has to take it on trust that something good will eventually turn up; it turns up on the first page. Indeed in *Brighton Rock* there is nothing else to equal its first chapter.

He usually plunges us at once into the centre of disaster, or somewhere near it. We are brought up against people, either in isolation or in a group, who are without belief or principle of conduct: the utterly uprooted, the drifting and the dispossessed; and they do not all come from social backwaters. The tragedy of many of his characters lies not only in the fact that they have gone off the rails, but that they have never known what rails are. Greene's range of feeling is particularly wide. He has written one great novel, *The Power and the Glory*, which is the culmination of all his powers and all his preoccupations. It is again about the hunted man: this time a priest in a communist state in Mexico round about 1930. It is essential in a story centred on the theme of pursuit that the reader should identify himself either with the pursuer or with the pursued; it is Greene's most signal triumph that even the " pagan " reader identifies himself with the priest. He is a bad priest, an irrepressible drunkard; and, though not a lecher, he has in a moment of abandonment begotten a child. It is a superb moment of tragic pathos when they meet, with the child, aged

CHRISTOPHER ISHERWOOD

GRAHAM GREENE

ROSAMOND LEHMANN

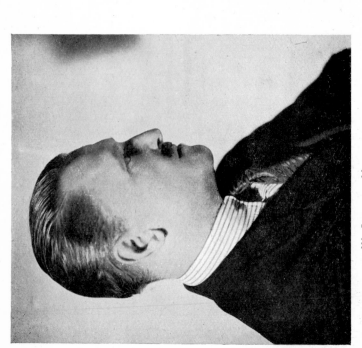

W. SOMERSET MAUGHAM

seven or eight, already on the way to a life of lewdness, tittering at him in the squalid jungle village. The priest is the most complex character Greene has so far drawn.

He said: " I don't know how to repent." That was true; he had lost the faculty. He couldn't say to himself that he wished his sin had never existed, because the sin seemed to him now so unimportant—and he loved the fruit of it. He needed a confessor to draw his mind slowly down the drab passages which led to horror, grief and repentance.

With wonderful, daring art, Greene draws his sinful priest, illuminated solely by the burden of God which he carries to the humble and the forcefully disinherited; this is his sole glory; even his final martyrdom is inglorious in its detail. Scarcely less remarkable is Greene's picture of the priest's opposite: the army lieutenant, the enforcer of False Order. For Greene, wholly without spiritual sympathy for him, yet presents him understandingly and with pity. Here he is, as he watches the children of the town:

It was for these he was fighting. He would eliminate from their childhood everything which had made him miserable, all that was poor, superstitious and corrupt. They deserved nothing less than the truth—a vacant universe and a cooling world, the right to be happy in any way they chose. He was quite prepared to make a massacre for their sakes—first the Church and then the foreigner and then the politician—even his own chief would one day have to go. He wanted to begin the world again with them, in a desert.

Important among Greene's books before *The Power and the Glory* are *England Made Me*, *It's a Battlefield* and *Brighton Rock*. The last of these is terrifying in its remorseless execution ; it sets out with the high aim of asserting the superiority of the knowledge of good and evil over the belief in mere right and wrong. Yet here the strength of Greene's initial beliefs seems to leave him nothing to discover while writing the book; in consequence the reader discovers nothing either. Much of the book is as brilliant as anything Greene has done; but at times there is an almost hysterical overemphasis of the basic contrast.

Greene has produced only an entertainment, *The Ministry of Fear*, since *The Power and the Glory*; it is the best of his entertainments, excellent in its evocation of bombed London and in the variety of its scene.   And it is remarkable in Greene's development as showing an increasing feeling for human love. *The Power and the Glory* blew such a great final chord to all that Greene had done before and seemed through art to solve so great a problem that one could have no conception what might come next.   The comparative gentleness of the hero and heroine in the later book perhaps gives us an indication; and the revulsion from " sex ", always strong in Greene, seems to have been put for a time aside.

Miss I. Compton-Burnett's characters dramatise a vestigial reminder of the struggle we have been discussing in connexion with Greene.   They are the weak and the strong; and if Miss Burnett's weak characters are not especially to be called good, we can certainly not deny evil to her strong ones.   The goodness in that small number of her men and women who possess it glows like a distant sun through a frosted window, and sooner or later it is invariably eclipsed.   Her books are about domestic crime, and not infrequently this includes murder; the cold villainy of some of her characters is doubtless the reason why her books have sometimes been compared to Elizabethan dramas; the comparison is certainly not without its point.   Her books have strongly-defined plots, and she herself has said:

As regards plots I find real life of no help at all.   Real life seems to have no plots.   And as I think a plot desirable and almost necessary, I have this extra grudge against life.   But I think there are signs that strange things happen, though they do not emerge.   I believe it would go ill with many of us, if we were faced with a strong temptation, and I suspect that with some of us it does go ill.

Miss Burnett begins with a fairly simple exercise in criminality in her first novel, *Pastors and Masters*.   (There is, in fact, an earlier novel, published many years before this, called *Dolores*, but it bears only slight relation to her present work.)   It is a book about schoolmasters and dons and the wives and sisters of these; it concerns a stolen manuscript which a university don tries to pass off as his own.   He is under the impression that the author of it is dead; it turns out to be by a living, intimate friend of his. But there is no quarrel. Wickedness is approached, but is not mentioned by that name. It is denounced by no-one; there is no punishment, no retribution, no remorse of conscience—*that*, least of all. There it is: simple, if not altogether straightforward. From novel to novel Miss Burnett proceeds, extending and expanding. When we get to her fourth book, *More Women than Men*, we find a character who uncoils herself as slowly and sinisterly as a serpent, and with a tongue no less smooth. Josephine Napier must be one of the wickedest characters in literature; yet she is wholly life-like.

Life-like, but not naturalistic. Miss Burnett has a manner of her own, which enabled her to emerge fully armed with *Pastors and Masters*: fully armed, and determined to carry out her campaigns only on her own elected terrain. Few early novels have been so lacking in blemish as *Pastors and Masters*; and it contains everything of the manner of her later novels. They are written almost entirely in concise, stylised conversations; colloquial contractions are rare. And we are deliberately given no sense of place. At the most, we may build up a certain impression of our own, as of the house and the lodge in *A Family and a Fortune*. The non-conversational passages are barely more than stage directions—though the characters are described in some detail on their first appearances. We are rarely left alone with them; and we are never asked to associate ourselves with their thoughts or their points of view. In *Pastors and Masters* one character *is* actually left alone for a moment; he devotes it to repeating to himself a speech he has just made, " with additions which had not occurred to him ". Such solitudes are rare in Miss Burnett's books; and rarely occupied so innocently.

When one has indicated the scope and nature of Miss Burnett's novels, and attempted to disarm the reader from being put off by a manner at first perplexing, and recommended them as entertainment, one has done pretty well all one can; but it should perhaps be added that, despite the conventionalised tone in which almost all her characters speak, no other living writer can manage so clearly to distinguish between the various members of a large cast —sometimes approaching twenty in number. The titles of her books, other than those already mentioned, are these: *Brothers and Sisters*, *Men and Wives*, *A House and Its Head*, *Daughters and Sons*, *Parents and Children*, *Elders and Betters*.

I have sometimes thought that Miss Elizabeth Bowen must have called one of her novels *Friends and Relations* in order to put the title out of Miss Burnett's reach. She is, however, a completely different kind of novelist, in feeling and in technique. Evil itself does not, so far, intrude on her world. It is not evil but the experience of others that corrodes the innocent people at the core of her books. And of the theme of innocence and experience she makes something closely approaching tragedy. It is the subject of her longest novel, *The Death of the Heart*; and one may discern the same thing in the novel which preceded it, *The House in Paris*. It is not an accident that in her little book on the English novelists she writes so well of three disparate authors: Jane Austen, Thomas Hardy and Henry James. She is not an imitative writer; but she has something in common with all of them. Her talent for social comedy, her eye for the socially absurd, recall—as they always will in an English writer—Jane Austen. She shares Hardy's love of atmosphere and shapely design. How soundly, for all their delicacy, her novels are constructed! And what Hardy will make of a woodland, a heath or a starve-acre farm, she will make of a house or a summer night. And—particularly in *The House in Paris* and in her later short stories—she shares James's love of seeing how a story can be persuaded into presenting the author with problems of artistry to solve. In her short stories she is noticeably fond of assembling a considerable number of characters and rendering them perfectly distinct in a comparatively short space of time. Like James again, she has a curiosity about the supernatural. It is not the same as belief; and she confines it to her short stories.

Her prose style has great subtlety; without being over-self-conscious, she has an awareness and a wit which enable her to know exactly where a sentence may demand a distortion from the conventional norm; and a poetic gift of concentrating the emotions of a scene, or a sequence of thoughts, or even a moral, into an

ELIZABETH BOWEN

ROBERT GRAVES

GEORGE ORWELL

V. S. PRITCHETT

unforgettable sentence or phrase. Her fiction during the war has been confined to short stories, of which she has published two impressive collections; *Look at all those Roses* and *The Demon Lover*. They possess the qualities of her novels, but inevitably the atmosphere in her short stories is richer and more concentrated. The more elaborate of them—*A Love Story* and *Summer Night* in the earlier volume, *The Inherited Clock*, *The Happy Autumn Fields* and *Ivy Gripped the Steps* in the later one—suggest the climaxes or the elements of novels, though in a necessarily muted or diminished form; but their "point" is always characteristic of the short story, and since it is their atmosphere which moulds them, and at times even brings them into existence (a fact which again reminds one of poetry), one does not think of them as truncated novels.

If I had to choose a book which most gave the feeling of war-time England I should choose *The Demon Lover*; the war, and the subtly degrading effect of the war, hold these stories together as a collection, and there is no story in the book which does not convey that feeling of the deterioration of the spirit which, when the tumult, and the shouting, and the self-deception subside, is seen to be war's residue. That which is squalid in peace-time—the adultery in the story *Pink May*, for example—accretes to itself an even sadder squalor in war. This is not to deny the heroism called for by war. It is to see something darker, beyond it: "with nothing left but our brute courage we shall be nothing but brutes".

This feeling is implicit in the most remarkable of her later stories, *The Happy Autumn Fields*, where by a supernatural dislocation of time the past and the present confront each other. Mary, the girl in the bombed house, who has caught two glimpses of an earlier world, is left lamenting:

We only know inconvenience now, not sorrow. Everything pulverises so easily because it is rot-dry; one can only wonder that it makes so much noise. The source, the sap must have dried up, or the pulse must have stopped, before you and I were conceived. So much flowed through people; so little flows through us. . . . I am left with a fragment torn out of a day, a day I don't even know where or when; and now how am I to help laying that like a pattern against the poor stuff of everything else?

—Alternatively, I am a person drained by a dream. I cannot forget the climate of those hours. Or life at that pitch, eventful—not happy, no, but strung like a harp.

James's comment about the past would have been different; but he did not live in our present.

IV

I have mentioned James a good deal in connexion with Miss Bowen. It is convenient here to mention one of the most remarkable novels published in England in recent years: Miss Rosamond Lehmann's *The Ballad and the Source*, which has also been strongly influenced by James. It is best approached through its title. A ballad is a poem based on an incident in history; it usually comes down to us in several versions, often contradictory; the source it derives from, the original action, grows perpetually more remote, as time and repeated narration distort and perhaps invert it. So it is with Mrs. Jardine's history in this novel. The story is told by a young child, to whom various aspects of Mrs. Jardine's story are confided by different people. To the child she appears as an embodiment of goodness and wisdom; she appears not otherwise to herself. The author's problem is to reveal Mrs. Jardine's vengefulness, through the medium of someone who does not perceive it, and at the same time to present its tragic origins, and the perversities it succeeds in transmitting to others. (The suggestion is also present that wickedness is an insanity of the sane; and that the offspring of the wicked may be truly insane.) It must not be forgotten that the word " source " has a double meaning: it is also, in Mrs. Jardine's words: " the quick spring that rises in illimitable depths of darkness and flows through every living thing from generation to generation. Sometimes the source is vitiated, choked. Then people live frail, wavering lives, their roots cut off from what should nourish them. That is what happens to people when love is betrayed—murdered." The words in Mrs. Jardine's mouth are self-righteous, and full of *arrière-pensée*. But they are the germ of the book; and it is a curious stroke of dramatic rightness that she should speak them.

The telling of the book is admirable, though there seems to me a certain flaw in the over-carefulness with which the personalities of the narrators are delineated. James, of course, would have let all the characters talk alike, and it is perhaps a genuine dissatisfaction with that method that makes Miss Lehmann over-naturalise her characters. The manners of the old nurse and the Scottish aunt, amusing in themselves, are nevertheless something of a distraction. At the same time the characterisation of the children does enable Miss Lehmann to achieve, in the last pages of the book, a poignant sense of their contaminated growth; and this also has its place in the general scheme.

The subject of *The Ballad and the Source* suggests that we turn aside for a time from particular writers, and note how often in the contemporary novel—not only in Britain—the theme of childhood recurs. Almost every important English writer of the moment has essayed to treat it. The reason is perhaps to be sought in the growing acceptance of the importance which is attached to childhood and infancy by psychology. But this only accounts for a little; there are other things, more consciously apprehensible. In a world of darkness we learn to hug that memory of comparative light. A child may be unhappy, but it is never wholly so; its happiness is not the mere absence of pain, and it has an innocence which the happiness of adult life is too complex to have. It is natural to turn and attempt to recapture and understand and detail that lost possibility of Eden.

I am not suggesting that childhood is a bed of roses; and if I were asked to point to recent accounts which give the truest version of the facts of childhood, I should point to Mr. Denton Welch's two sensational studies, *Maiden Voyage* and *In Youth is Pleasure*: the nightmare, the guilt, the secret acts, the obsessional sexual phantasies which I suppose no childhood is free from: they are all here, described with a frankness which makes the adult reader conscious of how much his memory omits to retain. These books are witty, pathetic, dramatic case-books; and in many ways—the hero's artistic knowledge may be instanced—the case Mr. Welch is dealing with is a special one. But they remind the novel-reader of how much the novelist is inclined to omit; and one is only slightly reassured by the recollection that omission is a part of the artistic process.

There were of course many novels about childhood before the war: for example, the comparatively direct narratives of John Hampson's *O Providence*, Stephen Spender's *The Backward Son* and Graham Greene's *The Basement Room*. Earlier, there was one dazzling masterpiece in Richard Hughes's *A High Wind in Jamaica*. They all show how far we have progressed from the children of Dickens and the " young barbarians " of Meredith; perhaps the children in Hardy's *Tess* and *Jude* have forced us on; certainly those of Henry James have.

Several particular books of recent years stand out as being adult books with children as the chief protagonists. First, Joyce Cary's *A House of Children*, which is a kind of lyrical symphony, and is told with an apparent disregard for chronology: although the characters develop and undergo the sudden striking transformations typical of childhood, and although incidents emerge and affect the action, it is the confusion and coexistence of our memories of different phases of childhood that the book so perfectly recaptures. The author employs long digressions as the various children and aspects of childhood come up for fresh treatment. The incidents are well chosen, and the author permits himself a modest climax in the form of an elopement. But it is the sense of growth and the observation of a child's capacity for change that are most convincing. "Anketel", Cary says of one character, " had been told of his former clever inventions, and now he imitated them. This made him unpopular, and he was accused of showing off, so that he became still more cut off and more affected. . . ." And so the child becomes lonely and miserable; he disappears from the scene, but seventy pages later we find that " he had changed from a bored, peevish affected child, a nuisance to everybody, into a friendly and sensible little boy ".

Then there is L. P. Hartley's *The Shrimp and the Anemone*, which is comic in manner but full of terror in its implications. It is the story of Orestes and Electra told in terms of infancy. Eustace, a trusting, intelligent and affectionate little boy, is continually manœuvred by Hilda, his elder sister, into feeling that he is in some way responsible for her happiness. Such a situation, with its many possible variants, is a common plight of childhood, and if in later life it is forgotten, it is only because the memory of it is not easy to bear. No particular blame attaches to Hilda. Eustace adores her, and she would give her life for him; but they are victims of a spiritual mechanism beyond their control; and we are left to suppose that eventual control of it is by no means likely, and might even be rejected: for how can Eustace, the shrimp, " bear to rob the anemone of its dinner "? Mr. Hartley's picture of childhood is, in fact, no less than a microcosm of the adult world, with its paralysing presentation of moral choices. It is lively, beautifully written, and without sentimentality.

The masterpiece of childhood—and one of the finest works of art in contemporary fiction—is a recently concluded trilogy by Forrest Reid. In chronological order of action the three books are: *Young Tom*, *The Retreat* and *Uncle Stephen*; they were, in fact, written in the reverse order, and I suspect that it is better to read them in that order, so that Tom, the hero, gets younger as one goes on. Reid was born in Belfast; and he has given an exquisite account of his own childhood and youth in an autobiography, *Apostate*, which is interesting to put beside the *Young Tom* trilogy: it reveals how very little, except for his tastes, Tom has in common with his author. And though any book about childhood is bound to seem autobiographical, even when it is not so, the extent of the invention in these books is a triumph for Mr. Reid.

In each of them a conflict of a serious order is dramatised through Tom and his surroundings. The conflict between imagination and science, between truth and information, is seen as a theme in *Young Tom* and *The Retreat*; in the latter book, fear—symbolised by a cat—and the destruction of fear, also have their place. The theme of *Uncle Stephen* is sacred and profane love, and is described as such by its author in *Private Road*, an excellent account of the experiences, phantasies, dreams and artistic processes that have brought his books into being. Like other readers, I find *Uncle Stephen*, despite its greater complexity and range, less satisfying than the two books which succeed it. I suspect that one is always vaguely perplexed when a novelist is rather evasive about physical relationships; but these are not in question in *The Retreat* and *Young Tom*, and in these the narrative acquires an unexampled purity and simplicity. It is undeniable that Mr. Reid can successfully treat only one subject: little boys. Anyone over sixteen seems beyond his scope; so that he is a writer far too little read. Nevertheless, *Young Tom* has been widely popular, and has won the respected honour of the Tait Black Memorial Prize. No living writer·commands a more beautiful prose style.

V

At least two other novelists writing in English today are worth considering in some detail: Joyce Cary and Henry Green. I have indeed already referred to Cary's *A House of Children*. Cary is one of the outstanding novelists of today. I have coupled him with Henry Green for no other reason than that they both have, as no other writers of their time have, a curiously wide variety. One could call them versatile, if that did not faintly suggest that their talents were mainly such as could be easily adapted to other people's models. The truth is rather that they both allow, or encourage, each new subject they approach to set for them a new problem of treatment. With Henry Green it is largely a question of style— of language. With Cary it is something else. The spirit and temperament of each of his books are different—and this is so even when his books fall into groups or phases. In this he is like a painter, ·and it is not altogether surprising to find that he studied art (in Paris and Edinburgh) long before becoming a novelist. He began to write much later than most novelists, and only after he had already had a varied career, including war service and two spells of political service in Africa.

His first book, *Aissa Saved*, rewritten many times, was published in 1930. His first group of novels derives—with the exception of *Castle Corner*—from his African experiences. His capacity for absorbing himself in his characters and in their *milieu* is unparalleled (save perhaps in Henry Green) in contemporary literature. He reminds us, if of anyone, of Defoe, who achieved a similar identification with his characters, and who had an enormous capacity for giving an apparently autobiographical inflection to incidents that were pure inventions. The picture of the ill-fated African clerk, Mister Johnson, in the novel of that name, is a brilliant piece of clairvoyance. We do not merely watch a " character " whose actions and reactions are discontinuous and irresponsible; we become that character. He is never a creature merely *observed*, and merely seen as funny or pathetic. Mr. Cary's objectivity is of a kind seen nowhere else in the modern English novel.

There is a similar transference of the reader's feeling into the centre of the action of a novel in Mr. Cary's next phase: his two contrasted novels about childhood. *A House of Children* has already been mentioned. *Charley is My Darling* is an even more remarkable work. It is about a group of slum children evacuated to a Devonshire village in the first year of the war. It ends in a tragedy of terrible poignancy; but its manner through the greater part of its length is comic to the point of being farcical. The scene where a group of children pause on a moonlight walk, and, carried away by a spirit of pure scientific curiosity, examine and compare each other's behinds for the residual effects of beating, is a truly memorable one.

Cary's last three books—*Herself Surprised*, *To be a Pilgrim* and *The Horse's Mouth*—are intended by the author to be a trilogy (though the three books are independent of each other) dealing with " English history, through English eyes, for the last sixty years ". *Herself Surprised* is a picture of working-class womanhood, *To be a Pilgrim* is a study of a Protestant lawyer, the offspring of wealthy landed parents. In some ways this book, though less spectacular than *The Horse's Mouth*, is Cary's best work. He manages two concurrent stories, of the past and the present, with great virtuosity; but the most remarkable thing in the book is the song of Protestantism which, as the title from Bunyan implies, resounds throughout it. Cary himself has said that England is "so essentially protestant in character that its whole political life is rooted in evangelical tradition". The idea of a "spirit of English history" is as repugnant to me as it is to most Englishmen; but if I had to choose one book to represent it with truth and dignity, I should choose this.

The Horse's Mouth is a study of a painter, but Gulley Jimson, its rowdy, dishonest, outrageous hero, represents more than the English artist. He is presented as a nuisance, and as a grotesque —his farcical passion for making mendacious telephone calls is a stroke of genius—but he does profoundly represent the visionary, obsessed artist who can never be popular except among a few of his contemporaries till after he is dead. In all of these books Cary has succeeded in eliminating himself—the aim of the author of *Finnegans Wake*. Wilcher, the lawyer of *To be a Pilgrim*, dogmatically expresses views with which we alternately agree and disagree: it is nowhere possible to feel sure what Cary's own opinions are. He has gifts of prolificacy and diversity in excess of any other contemporary novelist; I feel he may prove to be the one great novelist now writing in English.

Henry Green's first novel, *Blindness*, was written while he was still a schoolboy at Eton; it was published in 1926, and it remains astonishingly readable; its author's characteristic preoccupation with technique is already to be seen in it. In his autobiography, *Pack My Bag*, Green describes how, after leaving Oxford, he felt compelled to immerse himself in the life of the working class, and for several years he worked in his father's factory in Birmingham, living the life of a working man and writing in the evenings. The product of this time is a novel called *Living*, deliberately mannered in style, and written in Birmingham dialect, but again a novel of promise. It may be added that Green has not remained a factory worker; his name figures prominently in the Directory of Directors; before and during the war he was a member of the Auxiliary Fire Service, and he fought throughout the blitz on London.

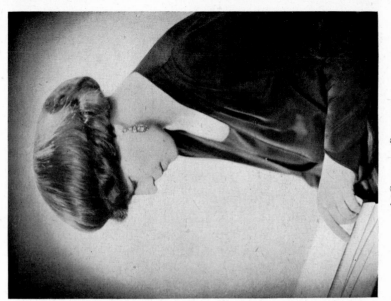

FORREST REID

I. COMPTON-BURNETT

JOYCE CARY

WILLIAM PLOMER

In his last three novels, *Party Going, Caught* and *Loving*, a definite design, almost a view of life, emerges. The books differ greatly from each other in setting: *Party Going* is about a party of rich young people marooned in the hotel of a London railway station by a fog which for the space of a few hours prevents their departure for a holiday in Europe; *Caught* is about the Auxiliary Fire Service during the waiting period before the blitz on London; *Loving* is about a group of servants in a castle in Ireland during the time when the country was expecting a German invasion. All of these books are unusual and arresting in style, *Caught* being the most direct and the most dramatic. But *Loving* seems to me the best and most subtle of Green's novels so far. It begins and ends with traditional fairy-story phrases: " Once upon a time " and " happily ever after ". But there is no fairy story between them, and it is not a romantic world that Green draws, though it has all the appanages of a fairy story: the great castle, the vanishing ring, the peacocks, the doves. But they are all the purposeful inversion of true fairy-story magic. The story is mainly about the servants' hall, and the principal character in the book is the housemaid, Edith. Three people are in love with her; and she herself is in love with Raunce, the butler. One morning she goes into her mistress's bedroom to draw the curtains; she discovers her mistress, whose husband is away in the army, in bed with a lover. She withdraws, horrified into speech-lessness. About this scene the whole book, comically and pathetic-ally, revolves. It is talked about in the servants' quarters at great length; it is a point on which all the emotions of the principal characters—who are all in some way frustrated—centre. But it is a point they never reach. This central incident has its parallel in *Caught*, where there is a scene in which a madwoman abducts a child; this scene also becomes a focal point in the book. *Caught* is doubtless a more serious novel than *Loving*; but the new novel is more successfully done, and its characters are more brilliantly interwoven with one another. An emotional Black Hole of Calcutta is the theme of both books—and of *Party Going* as well. Perhaps no atmospheres in life are quite so intense and concentrated as those of Mr. Green's expectant Fire Service and of his expectant

Irish castle. But this is what, in a book, one requires them to be. *Loving* achieves a particularly satisfying unity of atmosphere; the sense of an evanescent world is brilliantly captured. Each of Green's books sets him a new problem in literary manners; each of them is novel and fresh, and one is always set guessing at the announcement of a new one.

VI

In talking about novels on the subject of childhood, I have hinted that they may perhaps represent an honourable escape from present-day life. Alas for the critic of contemporary fiction, there are only too many writers who are quite content to face the music, and even to swell its noise. We may ignore those among the older novelists who have merely found the war to be grist to their zestful mills. We cannot, however, overlook young novelists in the same way. It is inevitable that they should have made aspects of the war their subject; it is in war-time that they have grown into the beginning of their novel-writing period. It is naturally difficult at the moment to assess the value of their work; we can only be sure that in the nature of things few of their books will survive their decade, if indeed they totter as far as the end of it. But among those who have treated the war, or, if not the war, the violence and distortions attendant on our own time, two young novelists stand out: F. L. Green and Nigel Balchin, who have each succeeded in making more than one good novel out of the material immediately around them.

F. L. Green (the reader may well believe Green to be an occupational name for novelists in England) was born in Portsmouth in 1902. He is partly Irish by descent, and Northern Ireland, where he lives, is the frequent setting of his books. Since the beginning of the war he has published a book every year. He made an immediate success with *On the Night of the Fire*. His books are unusual for the rapidity of their action and the diversity of their characters. He is fond of the hunted man as a character, and not unnaturally he is sometimes compared with Graham Greene. The comparison is said to please neither of these authors.

Though violence is often his theme, it is not a sadistic obsession with him, and it is part of his gift that peace, the longed-for opposite of violence, should always be implicit as a desire in the hearts of his characters. Green is a realist, but he chooses at the same time to generalise his themes by half-isolating them from the immediate facts of history. In *A Song for the Angels* the Germans are the enemy but the country they attack is unidentifiable; it could be any country. His best book is his latest, *Odd Man Out*. It is about a man called Johnny, the leader of a revolutionary organisation in Belfast; he kills a man in a struggle during a raid on a linen-mill, and is himself mortally wounded. The design of the story is simple but extremely effective; and it provides Green with a framework into which he can fit a large number of diverse scenes, while Johnny wanders and is pursued through the dark November night. The long and dreadful scene in the pub is a masterpiece in itself and there is a brilliant succession of minor characters, each seen in only one episode. The major characters leave some doubts in the mind, however, and it is certainly in the presentation of smaller people that Green excels. *On the Edge of the Sea*, an earlier and slighter novel than *Odd Man Out*, is made up of minor characters and is excellently done. It is breath-takingly exciting, and its picture of two Nazi thugs on a mission to Northern Ireland, miserably loathing the undisciplined freedom of the scene, and longing for a dictated and directed life, is particularly good.

War is a quotidian nightmare, and to read most war books is to share the nightmare and nothing else. But we may gratefully remember books like Nigel Balchin's *Darkness Falls from the Air* and *The Small Back Room*, which are brilliantly set in war-time civil service organisations. Balchin's gifts are very boldly defined ones: ability to control a large number of characters, high nervous tension in the evolution of the plot, and a capacity for naturalistic dialogue. His most popular book, *The Small Back Room*, is about a difficult personal relationship, the squabbling, jealousy and frustration in a scientific war research department, and the efforts to solve the mystery of a lethal German booby-trap; the material may sound either unpromising or unoriginal, but Balchin weaves his three themes together into an intense, amusing and moving novel. It is the work of a novelist who is confident that his subject-matter approaches the tragic, and Balchin treats it with great conviction. The writing at times suggests a hang-over from the tough-senti-mental American schools; but this fault has disappeared in such short narrative passages as occur in Balchin's latest book, *Mine Own Executioner*, an excellent novel, mainly in dialogue, about a psycho-analyst faced not only with the tormenting problems of his patients but also with his own failing love, for which his science has no cure. Balchin's treatment of his women characters seems to arouse a dislike in women readers comparable with that aroused by Somerset Maugham. To a male reader they seem wholly con-vincing; and " Rhino ", the neglected wife in *Mine Own Executioner*, is surely an enchanting portrait.

To read Balchin is to remember that the younger novelists have had to live through what they describe, and that problems of style, technique and angle are not usually solvable in conditions of ener-getic strain. During the war years, if a young novelist has been conscious of the fact that *writing* is itself a problem, his tendency has frequently been to write in the staccato manner of the early Hemingway. This, a kind of hectic impressionism, is also char-acteristic of some well-known older writers such as James Hanley, whose *No Directions*, a wild novel about a single air raid and its effect on a house full of people, exemplifies both his faults and his virtues. It is an extremely confusing and not a particularly com-pelling book to read, but scenes of great reality stand out and the bare hints of tragedy are unforgettable; and Hanley always has his surprising bursts of poetry: the description of an air-raid warning is a wonderful *cadenza*. Hanley is also an outstanding short story writer.

Many other war books could be mentioned which have shown promising writers emerging: such books as *F.S.P.* (the initials of the Field Security Police), a book about army life up to Dunkirk, by A. Gwynne-Browne, who penetrates beyond Hemingway to

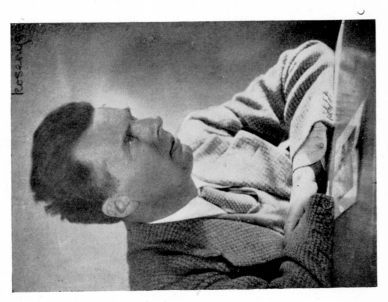

EVELYN WAUGH

ALDOUS HUXLEY

NIGEL BALCHIN

F. L. GREEN

Gertrude Stein and, by no means unsuccessfully, adapts her to his purpose. Another and more brilliant book about the army before war became total is *Then a Soldier*, by Geoffrey Cottrell, a comic writer of rare perception and ability.

Comic books about the war have, in fact, appeared with healthy and refreshing regularity. One's gratitude for them has rendered one indifferent about their justice, probability or accuracy; it is only with pleasure that one recalls Lord Berners's satirical little tale of Oxford life, *Far from the Madding War*; G. W. Stonier's *Shaving through the Blitz*, which is right inside the madding war; and the stories in Osbert Sitwell's *Open the Door!* In more recent months there has appeared George Orwell's delectable *Animal Farm*, which breathes new life into the deadest of literary forms. And from the early years of the war one remembers Rose Macaulay's *And No Man's Wit*, a novel about Spain between Franco's victory and the outbreak of the general war; it is a brilliant mixture of discourse and fantasy. One of the best of contemporary comic writers—though he cannot be regarded simply as comic—is V. S. Pritchett; Pritchett was already, before the war, the author of two serious novels, *Nothing Like Leather* and *Dead Man Leading*; during the war he has acquired an enormous reputation as a short story writer. He is also one of our most distinguished literary critics. His short stories, which usually deal with lower middle-class life, are almost the exact opposite in method of those of Elizabeth Bowen; though both writers are characterised by a similar wit and sensibility. But Miss Bowen, as I have hinted, starts with her setting, and the characters emerge from it: the romantic method. Pritchett is a classicist: he starts always with his characters, whom he observes minutely as he confronts them with a situation. I imagine that the best of his stories written in this manner, *Sense of Humour*, *The Sailor*, *The Saint* and certain others, are as certainly assured of a permanent place in literature as anything I have mentioned in these pages. Ultimately Pritchett will demand the novel for the full expression of his faculty, and his next novel is awaited with great curiosity—the more so since he has written acutely about many of the great novelists in a book of essays called (a little too archly) *In My Good Books*. If I had space, there are many authors I should more than mention; many English readers would justly deplore the fact that such writers as Robert Graves, H. E. Bates, Desmond Hawkins, Frank Tilsley, Mary Renault, Robert Goodyear, Alun Lewis, Bruce Marshall, Charles Williams, Glyn Jones, Rhys Davies and others are mentioned here only by name. But I propose to devote the rest of my space to other and more questionable omissions, and to certain writers who have so far been absent from these pages through no fault of mine.

VII

I said at the outset that I did not propose to discuss best-sellers; but the talents of three very popular novelists force themselves to be noticed. They are Somerset Maugham, Aldous Huxley and Evelyn Waugh. A critic who has to economise on space is grateful that they have all written novels about approximately the same subject during the war. In a disastrously torn world their common theme is not surprising. *The Razor's Edge*, *Time Must Have a Stop* and *Brideshead Revisited* all have heroes in whom the principal aspect stressed by their authors is a relationship to God. I do not think that any of these writers would much approve of the others, though Maugham, with the widest psychological knowledge, might be the most tolerant.

Maugham's novel, in construction and prose style, seems to me infinitely the best of the three. Its virtuosity calls attention to itself rather pointedly every now and then, but after all, the virtuosity is there. The book has its falsities, and these centre chiefly where they are least easy to overlook—in the drawing of Larry, the hero, and of Larry's circumstances; the purity so apparent to Larry's friends is not apparent to the reader, and it is difficult to think of £800 a year as being a razor's edge. Nevertheless the people round Larry are, in general, excellently drawn, and Elliot Templeman, the worldly Catholic convert, is a masterpiece who in himself will keep the book alive. The book's impudent and apparently casual evolution is astonishingly satisfying.

Intellectually, the most brilliant of these books is Huxley's; but to me his slovenly narrative style, his by now mechanical, amused disgust at bodily functions and his still-adolescent daring make the first half of his book all but unreadable; however, the old man's sensations on the threshold of the after-life are vastly entertaining; this is the part of the book in which Huxley is himself really interested, and the only part to which he appears to have given more than perfunctory attention. It is wholly characteristic of Huxley that the old man should die in a water-closet.

Brideshead Revisited has its own faults, but—possibly because to a European, Christianity still appears precise, and other religions appear vague—its general design, boldly conceived and executed, is more impressive than that of the other two novels. It is about the workings of the divine spirit through an aristocratic Catholic family in England; Sebastian, the hero, is a homosexual drunkard; his sister, Julia, is an adulteress; his father is an apostate living in Venice with a mistress. Their lives are almost wholly sinful, yet Waugh presents them as capable of redemption because in the recesses of their hearts is an acknowledgement that they are, even in their worst moments, still within reach of the idea of God; as those outside the Church are not. Waugh seems to me to lack religious feeling, yet somehow one accepts the theme of his novel. Its most notable flaws lie in the strange tastelessness of its snobbery, and its occasional lapses into the manner of the novelette.

Waugh's social beliefs are really like those of Yeats, who wanted to see " great wealth in the hands of a few, and petitioners at the gate ". This mattered little in the end with Yeats, because art mattered more; Waugh is indifferent to art, and a reactionary point of view which might have produced great liveliness declines in him into irritated pettiness. *Brideshead Revisited* is his first serious novel, though serious hints have been often enough implicit in his earlier farces. He has always been a superb funny writer; he can make one laugh even when one hates to do so. His picture of the evacuated slum children, the Connollys, in *Put Out More Flags* is an example of what

C 2

I mean; one has only to place the Connollys beside the children in Cary's *Charley is My Darling* to realise how poor a thing satire is by the side of comedy and tragedy.

The patient reader will have observed that my sympathies with these three writers are, to say the least, imperfect. But it would be unpardonable to omit them: it would be equally unpardonable to omit to name several others with whom I have no sympathy at all: writers who have been greatly applauded by critics whom I respect. So that I am deeply conscious that another critic might well have devoted much space to such writers as R. C. Hutchinson and L. H. Myers; or to those writers who, like Rex Warner, have come under the widespread influence of Kafka. But every critic must sometimes hesitate, and I hesitate here. I can see that Hutchinson has a remarkable gift for submerging himself completely in a foreign country (as, for instance, France in *Shining Scabbard*) and writing of its life as though he were a native author—sometimes a badly translated one. But I cannot see anything else of great interest in his books. With Myers it is different; he is a philo-sophical writer and the views he expounds in his famous tetra-logy, *The Near and the Far*, are of great interest; but I can feel far less warmth for this book as a novel than I can for his earlier works, *Strange Glory* and *The " Clio "*. I admire a good deal of Kafka (his *America* seems to me one of the great novels of the world); but his manner—the manner of dreams—of presenting the incon-sequent as though it were a logical and natural sequence, is appro-priate only to his own material, which is mainly concerned with man's irrational sense of guilt; and his symbolism has been confused, at any rate by English writers, with a low form of allegory.

I cannot end this survey without a reference to certain important absentees, as they may be called; I refer to those writers who were, before the war, regarded as possessing great promise and who, for whatever reason, have produced little or no work during it. This does not mean they are absent from one's view of the con-temporary novel; one always thinks a little way into the future, and one is cheered to hear that new novels are " on the way " from many other writers than those I have named here. Little has been heard during the war of a talented group of young writers from the Midlands: John Hampson, whose *Saturday Night at the Greyhound* is deservedly well known outside England; Walter Allen, whose *Innocence is Drowned*, is a moving story of working-class and university life in a provincial town; and Leslie Halward, a gifted and original short story writer. All of these writers have several books to their credit; but the war has apparently impeded their progress, and one has heard little of them.

Of three other novelists, far more widely known, one has heard nothing at all; or at any rate one has had no new novels from them. Richard Hughes, whose early novel, *A High Wind in Jamaica*, has already been mentioned, has produced no novel during the war; though *In Hazard*, itself a brilliant achievement, comparable with —and not written without recollection of—Conrad's *Typhoon*, appeared in 1938. William Plomer, a novelist and poet whose sole prose work during the war has been an accomplished autobiography, *Double Lives*, is one of the most versatile figures in present-day literature. He has perhaps produced no wholly satisfying novel, in spite of great insight into character and a power to manage dialogue; he inclines carefully to describe a situation rather than to dramatise it, and his short stories so far show him at his best; his power of evoking an exotic scene and atmosphere is not surpassed by any living novelist. His characters are almost always the uprooted people of society, misfits whom he describes with mingled pity, irony and malice. The same gifts are also to be seen in Christopher Isherwood, who migrated to America shortly before the war and who has remained there till recently as a devotee of Yoga; no hint of mysticism is to be found in his novels or stories; the later ones, about pre-Hitler Berlin, are characterised by a lucid wit and objectivity and by a deceptively simple precision of style.

These three writers, Hughes, Plomer and Isherwood, are among the most gifted and promising English writers of their time; it is with a hope for the return of their gifts and for the fulfilment of their promise that I can best end. Looking through these pages from time to time as I have written them, I have felt more than ever cheered by the absence of " movements " in the contemporary English novel. Many of our novelists are socialists, almost all of them are realists; I am glad of both of these things, but I am more glad that we have no " socialist realists ". And though beside the novels of Miss Compton-Burnett " existentialism " sounds like the merry chanting of a troupe of Boy Scouts, we have no existentialists pure and simple. I can see, as I said at the beginning, no tendencies: only a considerable number of novelists, helped by one another at certain points, but in the last resort each making his or her own way.

SELECT BIBLIOGRAPHY

N.B. Several critical works on the five authors mentioned as "background" have been published since 1939 and I mention a few of them here. There have been three books on Hardy. Those by Henry Nevinson (*Thomas Hardy*) and Edmund Blunden (*Thomas Hardy*: English Men of Letters Series) are inconsiderable, though the former contains a credible picture of Hardy as a person. David Cecil's *Hardy the Novelist* is the best study of the novels that has yet appeared, valuable both for its insistence on the poet as novelist and for its comparisons of Hardy with other novelists. No book on James was published in Britain during the war, but the Oxford University Press has since issued here an American study, *Henry James: The Major Phase*, by F. O. Mathiesson. Two other American critical studies are relevant to these pages: *James Joyce*, by Harry Levin, and *E. M. Forster*, by Lionel Trilling. There have been two studies called *Virginia Woolf*, one by Joan Bennett, the other by David Daiches; the former is by far the more important.

NIGEL BALCHIN—*No Sky* (1933); *Simple Life* (1934); *Lightbody on Liberty* (1937); *Income and Outcome* (1936); *Darkness Falls from the Air* (1942); *The Small Back Room* (1943); *Mine Own Executioner* (1945).

ELIZABETH BOWEN—*Encounters* (stories) (1923); *Ann Lee's* (stories) (1926); *The Hotel* (1927); *The Last September* (1929); *Joining Charles* (stories) (1929); *Friends and Relations* (1931); *To the North* (1932); *The Cat Jumps* (stories) (1934); *The House in Paris* (1935); *The Death of the Heart* (1938); *Look at all those Roses* (stories) (1941); *Bowen's Court* (family history) (1942); *Seven Winters* (autobiography) (1943); *The Demon Lover* (stories) (1945).

JOYCE CARY—*Aissa Saved* (1932); *An American Visitor* (1933); *The African Witch* (1936); *Castle Corner* (1938); *Mister Johnson* (1939); *Charley is My Darling* (1940); *A House of Children* (1941); *Herself Surprised* (1941); *To be a Pilgrim* (1942); *The Horse's Mouth* (1944); *The Moonlight* (1946).
Politics—*The Case for African Freedom* (1941); *Power in Men* (1939); *Process of Real Freedom* (1943).
Poem—*Marching Soldier* (1945).

I. COMPTON-BURNETT—*Dolores* (1913); *Pastors and Masters* (1925); *Brothers and Sisters* (1929); *Men and Wives* (1931); *More Women than*

Men (1933); *A House and Its Head* (1935); *Daughters and Sons* (1937); *A Family and a Fortune* (1939); *Parents and Children* (1941); *Elders and Betters* (1944).

E. M. FORSTER—Fiction: *Where Angels Fear to Tread* (1905); *The Longest Journey* (1907); *A Room with a View* (1908); *Howards End* (1910); *The Celestial Omnibus* (stories) (1911); *A Passage to India* (1924); *The Eternal Moment* (stories) (1928).

  Criticism, etc.—*A Letter to Madan Blanchard* (1931); *Introduction and Notes to the Aeneid of Virgil* (1906); *Alexandria, a History and a Guide* (1922); *Pharos and Pharillon* (1923); *Introduction and Notes to the Letters of Mrs. Eliza Fay* (1925); *Anonymity, an Enquiry* (1925); *Aspects of the Novel* (Clark Lectures, 1927); *Introduction to the Life of Crabbe* (1932); *Goldsworthy Lowes Dickinson* (1934); *What I Believe* (1939); *Abinger Harvest* (essays) (1936); *England's Pleasant Land* (Abinger pageant play) (1940); *Nordic Twilight* (war pamphlet) (1940); *Virginia Woolf* (Rede Lecture, 1941).

F. L. GREEN—*Julius Penton* (1934); *On the Night of the Fire* (1939); *The Sound of Winter* (1940); *Give us the World* (1941); *Music in the Park* (1942); *A Song for the Angels* (1943); *On the Edge of the Sea* (1944); *Odd Man Out* (1945); *A Flask for the Journey* (1946).

HENRY GREEN—*Blindness* (1926); *Living* (1929); *Party Going* (1939); *Pack My Bag* (1940); *Caught* (1943); *Loving* (1945).

GRAHAM GREENE—*The Man Within* (1929); *The Name of Action* (1930); *Rumour at Nightfall* (1931); *Stamboul Train* (1932); *It's a Battlefield* (1934); *England Made Me* (1935); *The Basement Room* (stories) (1935); *Journey Without Maps* (travel) (1936); *A Gun for Sale* (1936); *Brighton Rock* (1938); *The Lawless Roads* (travel) (1939); *The Confidential Agent* (1939); *The Power and the Glory* (1940); *British Dramatists* (criticism) (1942); *The Ministry of Fear* (1943).

JAMES HANLEY—*Drift* (1930); *The Last Voyage* (1931); *The German Prisoner* (1930); *A Passion before Death* (1930); *Boy* (1931); *Ebb and Flood* (1931); *Aria and Finale* (stories) (1932); *Captain Bottell* (1933); *The Furys* (1934); *Men in Darkness* (stories) (1931); *Stoker Bush* (1935); *The Maelstrom* (1935); *The Secret Journey* (1936); *The Wall* (1936); *Broken Water* (autobiography) (1937); *Grey Children: A Sociological Study* (1937); *Half an Eve* (stories) (1937); *Hollow Sea* (1938); *Soldiers Wind* (essays) (1938); *People are Curious* (stories) (1938); *Between the Tides* (essays) (1939); *Our Time is Gone* (1940); *The Ocean*

(1941); *No Directions* (1943); *At Bay* (stories) (1943); *Sailor's Song* (1943); *Crilley* (stories) (1945); *What Farrar Saw* (1945).

L. P. HARTLEY—*The Shrimp and the Anemone* (1944).

RICHARD HUGHES—*Gipsy Night* (poems) (1922); *The Sisters' Tragedy, and other Plays* (1924); *Poems by John Skelton* (edited) (1924); *A Moment of Time* (stories) (1926); *Confessio Juvenis* (poems) (1926); *Plays* (1928); *A High Wind in Jamaica* (*The Innocent Voyage*) (1929); *The Spider's Palace* (children's stories) (1931); *In Hazard* (1938); *Don't Blame Me* (children's stories) (1940).

ALDOUS HUXLEY—Novels: *Crome Yellow* (1921); *Antic Hay* (1923); *Those Barren Leaves* (1925); *Point Counter Point* (1928); *Brave New World* (1932); *Eyeless in Gaza* (1936); *After Many a Summer* (1939); *Time Must Have a Stop* (1944).
  Short Stories—*Limbo* (1920); *Mortal Coils* (1922); *Little Mexican* (1924); *Two or Three Graces* (1926); *Brief Candles* (1930).
  Essays, etc.—*On the Margin* (1923); *Along the Road* (1925); *Jesting Pilate* (1926); *Proper Studies* (1927); *Do What You Will* (1929); *Music at Night* (1931); *Texts and Pretexts* (anthology) (1932); *Beyond the Mexique Bay* (1934); *The Olive Tree, and other Essays* (1936); *Ends and Means* (1937); *The Perennial Philosophy* (1946).
  Poetry—*The Burning Wheel* (1916); *The Defeat of Youth* (1918); *Leda* (1920); *The Cicadas* (1931).
  Drama—*The World of Light* (1931).
  Biography—Edited, *The Letters of D. H. Lawrence* (1932); *Grey Eminence* (1941).

CHRISTOPHER ISHERWOOD—Fiction: *All the Conspirators* (1928); *The Memorial* (1932); *Mr. Norris Changes Trains* (1935); *Goodbye to Berlin* (1939); *Prater Violet* (1945).
  Plays—(All with W. H. Auden) *The Dog Beneath the Skin* (1935); *Ascent of F.6* (1937); *On the Frontier* (1938).
  Autobiography—*Lions and Shadows* (1938).
  Travel—*Journey to a War* (with W. H. Auden) (1939).

JAMES JOYCE (1882–1941)—*Chamber Music* (verses) (1907); *Dubliners* (stories) (1914); *A Portrait of the Artist as a Young Man* (1916); *Exiles* (play) (1918); *Ulysses* (1922); *Pomes Penyeach* (verses) (1927); *Finnegans Wake* (1939); *Stephen Hero* (1944);—Edited by T. S. Eliot: *Introducing James Joyce: A Selection of Joyce's Prose* (1942).

ROSAMOND LEHMANN—*Dusty Answer* (1927); *A Note in Music* (1930); *Invitation to the Waltz* (1932); *The Weather in the Streets* (1936); *No more Music* (play) (1939); *The Ballad and the Source* (1944); *The Gypsy's Baby, and other stories* (1946).

ROSE MACAULAY—*What Not* (1919); *Potterism* (1920); *Dangerous Ages* (1921); *Mystery of Geneva* (1922); *Told by an Idiot* (1923); *Orphan Island* (1924); *Crewe Train* (1926); *A Casual Commentary* (essays) (1925); *Keeping up Appearances* (1928); *Staying with Relations* (1930); *Some Religious Elements in English Literature* (1931); *They were Defeated* (1932); *John Milton* (biography) (1933); *Going Abroad* (1934); *The Minor Pleasures of Life* (anthology) (1934); *Personal Pleasures* (anthology) (1935); *I Would be Private* (1937); *The Writings of E. M. Forster* (criticism) (1938); *And No Man's Wit* (1940); *Life Among the English* (historical essay) (1942).

W. SOMERSET MAUGHAM—*Liza of Lambeth* (1897); *Mrs. Craddock* (1902); *The Land of the Blessed Virgin* (1905); *The Magician* (1908); *Of Human Bondage* (1915); *The Moon and Sixpence* (1919); *The Trembling of a Leaf* (1921); *On a Chinese Screen* (1922); *The Painted Veil* (1925); *The Casuarina Tree* (1926); *Ashenden* (1928); *The Gentleman in the Parlour* (1930); *Cakes and Ale* (1930); *First Person Singular* (1931); *The Narrow Corner* (1932); *Ah King* (1933); *Altogether* (stories) (1934); *Don Fernando* (1935); *Cosmopolitans* (stories) (1936); *Theatre* (1937); *The Summing Up* (autobiography) (1938); *Christmas Holiday* (1939); *The Mixture as Before* (1940); *Up at the Villa* (1941); *The Razor's Edge* (1944); *Then and Now* (1946). More than twenty plays.

GEORGE ORWELL—*Coming up for Air* (1939); *Down and Out in Paris and London* (travel) (1933); *Inside the Whale* (1940); *The Lion and the Unicorn* (1941); *Burmese Days* (1935); *Animal Farm* (1945).

WILLIAM PLOMER—*Turbott Wolfe* (1926); *I speak of Africa* (1927); *Paper Houses* (1929); *Sado* (1931); *The Fivefold Screen* (poems) (1932); *The Case is Altered* (1932); *Cecil Rhodes* (biography) (1933); *The Child of Queen Victoria* (1933); *The Invaders* (1934); *Ali the Lion* (1936); *Visiting the Caves* (poems) (1936); *Kilvert's Diary* (edited) (1938–40); *Selected Poems* (1940); *Double Lives* (autobiography) (1943); *The Dorking Thigh* (poems) (1945).

V. S. PRITCHETT—*Marching Spain* (1928); *Clare Drummer* (1929); *The Spanish Virgin* (1930); *Shirley Sanz* (1932); *Nothing Like Leather* (1935); *Dead Man Leading* (1937); *You Make Your Own Life* (1938); *In My Good Books* (criticism) (1942); *It May Never Happen* (1945).

FORREST REID—*The Bracknels, a Family Chronicle* (1911); *Following Darkness* (1912); *The Gentle Lover* (1913); *W. B. Yeats* (criticism) (1915); *At the Door of the Gate* (1915); *The Spring Song* (1916); *A Garden by the Sea* (1918); *Pirates of the Spring* (1919); *Pender Among the Residents* (1922); *Apostate* (1926); *Demophon* (1927); *Illustrators of the Sixties* (1928); *Walter de la Mare* (criticism) (1929); *Uncle Stephen* (1931); *Brian Westby* (1934); *The Retreat* (1936); *Peter Waring* (revised version of *Following Darkness*) (1937); *Private Road* (1940); *Retrospective Adventures* (essays) (1941); *Poems from the Greek Anthology* (1943); *Young Tom* (1944).

EVELYN WAUGH—*Rossetti* (1928); *Decline and Fall* (1928); *Vile Bodies* (1930); *Labels* (1930); *Remote People* (1932); *Black Mischief* (1932); *Ninety-Two Days* (1934); *A Handful of Dust* (1934); *Edmund Campion* (biography) (1935); *Waugh in Abyssinia* (1936); *Scoop* (1938); *Put Out More Flags* (1942); *Work Suspended* (1942); *Brideshead Revisited* (1945).

DENTON WELCH—*Maiden Voyage* (1943); *In Youth is Pleasure* (1945).

VIRGINIA WOOLF (1882–1941)—*The Voyage Out* (1915); *Night and Day* (1919); *Monday or Tuesday* (1921); *Jacob's Room* (1922); *The Common Reader* (criticism) (1925); *Mrs. Dalloway* (1925); *To the Lighthouse* (1927); *Orlando* (1929); *A Room of One's Own* (criticism) (1929); *The Waves* (1931); *The Common Reader: Second Series* (criticism) (1932); *Flush* (biography) (1933); *The Years* (1937); *Three Guineas* (essay) (1938); *Reviewing* (1939); *Roger Fry, a Biography* (1940); *Between the Acts* (1941); *The Death of the Moth* (miscellaneous essays) (1942); *A Haunted House* (stories) (1943).

British Book News, *a monthly list of new books and reprints, select, classified and annotated, will be sent without charge to residents outside Britain who apply to the* National Book League, 7 Albermarle Street, London, W.1.

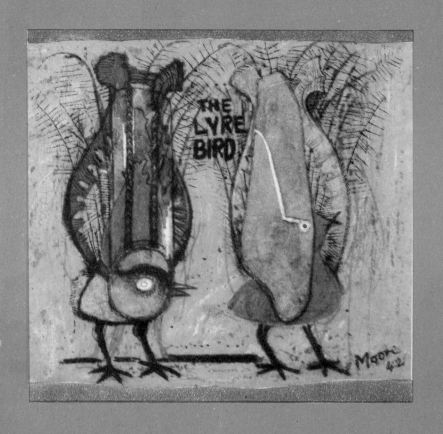

THE
LYRE
BIRD

Moore
42

POETRY

SINCE

1939

STEPHEN SPENDER